A PAT
YOUR FIRST YEAR
OF LEADING HUDDLE

HUDDLE
LEADER
GUIDE

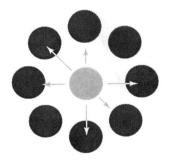

MIKE BREEN

For information, write to 3 Dimension Ministries, 14 Lincoln St, Greenville, SC 29601, USA or 3dmovements.com

First edition 2012
Second edition first printing 2017
Printed in United States
4 5 6 7 8 9 10 11 12 13 Printing/Year 15 14 13 12 11 10

Cover Design: Blake Berg
Editor/Interior Design: Pete Berg

ISBN: 978-0-9990039-0-9

3DM Publishing

3dmpublishing.com

CONTENTS

Part 3: After Year 1 + Appendix

PART 1

BEFORE
YOU BEGIN

PURPOSE OF THIS
LEADER GUIDE

This guide is a response to people who have asked for a more detailed resource as they begin to lead their first few Huddles. In the past, my teams and I were leery about putting out such a resource, because we didn't want to convey the idea that there is a magic formula to leading a Huddle. So let us say from the outset that **there is no perfect formula**.

However, we also think it is helpful to provide a basic framework for the first year of a Huddle. That's what you'll find here. At the same time, this guide is meant to teach you how to find freedom within that framework. This is another way of saying that each Huddle leader should discern the best way forward for their Huddle. Each Huddle, each leader, and each participant is different. Over 20+ years of leading Huddles and Huddle leaders, I have never seen a Huddle look like any other Huddles I have led. But there are also similarities in every Huddle based on values, principles, and practices that you find in this guide.

Our one caveat: This guide cannot compensate for you not having been in a Huddle where you were the participant. It is essential that you be in a Huddle before leading one. I can't emphasize that strongly or loudly enough.

I pray that you will find this revised version of the Huddle leader's guide to be a helpful resource that aids you during your first year of Huddle.

HOW TO USE THIS
LEADER GUIDE

This guide consists of three sections.

- Part 1 lays the foundation for Huddle, and gives an overview of the framework and how the freedom you can find within it, while also providing details you'll need to know heading into your first Huddle.

- Part 2 is the framework for the first year of a Huddle.

- Part 3 includes some additional notes as well as thoughts on how to lead Huddle once you've finished going through the LifeShapes and the framework provided here. It also includes the Appendix.

Take time to read through the entire guide before diving into your Huddle, because this guide contains many puzzle pieces that fit together into an integrated whole. Also, please note that throughout the book, you'll find strategic places for you to take notes via short exercises to help you discern the path God is taking your Huddle. Put these to good use.

You'll want to keep your copy of *Building a Discipling Culture* regularly have at your side, as it is a superb reference guide, particularly in Part 3 of the book, which goes into meticulous detail on how to lead Huddle. This revised guide coordinates with the third edition of that book, which was released in 2017.

There is also a revised Huddle participant guide that mirrors the framework in this book. It will be quite helpful for the people you are huddling.

Lastly, throughout this book you will find coaching tips that other leaders have found really helpful in leading Huddles. As I have often said before: "You'll make mistakes along the way—just make different ones than we've already made!"

WHAT IS
HUDDLE?

In a moment, let's begin with a bullet-point list defining a Huddle. But first, it's important to clearly state that a Huddle is a vehicle designed is for current or future leaders. Over 20 years, the discipleship movement that you and I are a part of has proven that if you disciple leaders well and give them the tools, vehicles, and principles to disciple, everyone in your church will be discipled. So as you begin the journey of leading a Huddle, remember that it's crucial for you to invite leaders into the discipling relationship with you.

HUDDLE IS:

- A place to directly disciple your current or future leaders in mission and discipleship
- A place to give and receive encouragement and accountability
- For a group of 4 to 10 people (we recommend starting with 4-6 people)

- Regular and consistent in its rhythm of meeting (at least every other week, but usually held weekly)

- Led by the Huddle leader

- Something you are invited into by the leader. This is not something people bring a friend to. If you lead a Huddle, then it is your Huddle, and you set the terms, including whom you choose to disciple and invite.

- A privilege, not a right

- Relaxed and fun. Laughter should happen regularly!

- Dependent on openness and honesty within the life of the Huddle

- Helping people answer two questions each time they meet:

  a. What is God saying to me?

  b. What am I going to do about it?

- For a season only, not forever. We tend to ask people to commit for a church ministry year at a time. Obviously, your current leaders remain in Huddles for as long as they are leading people, but you will want to shake things up from time to time.

- Measured by growth in maturity and fruitfulness of members

- Something that multiplies over time, as members start their own Huddles

Coaching Tip: Your Huddle will plateau and stall within 3-6 months if your participants aren't leading something. Without the opportunity to lead, Huddle becomes just another thing they do in an already busy life.

SPIRITUAL FORMATION PROCESS

PHASE ONE: LANGUAGE

As is thoroughly discussed in *Building a Discipling Culture*, language creates culture. LifeShapes is a powerful discipling language, and so this guide recommends focusing on this language during your first year of Huddle.

It's important to understand this language lays the foundation for everything else. It helps establish the biblical worldview of Jesus and gives people a lens to see the world in the way that Jesus did. Huddle is a tool for slowly teaching people this language. The first few months of Huddle are similar to learning basic Spanish. You have to know some of the nouns and pronouns and how to conjugate verbs before you can really start immersing yourself in the language and becoming fluent in it. It's all about the basics.

Learning the basics of the language is key, particularly as people learn to engage the two central questions:

A. What is God saying to me?

B. What am I going to do about it?

This is foreign for so many people. Most people don't even know how to hear and discern the voice of God, much less respond to it.

Jesus clearly establishes this foundation of language. On the first day of his ministry, he introduces the idea of the Kingdom. Very soon after that he delivers the Sermon on the Mount, exploring more fully the reality of the Kingdom of God. Everything that he teaches, every story he gives, and every action he makes is wrapped up in the language of the Kingdom of God. This language of the Kingdom put handles on truth so people could remember and understand. This should be the goal of the language you use in your Huddle as well.

PHASE TWO: RHYTHMS

This phase is about learning the rhythms of life that Jesus talks about in John 15—how there is an ever-swinging pendulum between rest and work that was written into our bodies from the creation of the world. Jesus is trying to draw out this principle: *We are designed to work from a place of rest; not rest from work.*

He makes it quite clear that real rest is found in him being connected to his Father. It is in times of rest that we not only receive the Father's life and energy, but also hear his voice.

Because so few people have ever sustained daily or weekly rhythms in their lives, it usually takes months for this to happen in the lives of the people in your Huddle. In order to do this, most people will need to start getting up early every day to spend time in scripture and prayer. Of course, this isn't how everyone will function, and that should be OK. It isn't law, and certainly some people don't start their day this way, but the experience of the movement tells us this is generally the case. The experience of Huddle leaders in the movement tells us that if we can win this first, all-important battle of the day, the other battles of the day go our way a lot easier.

This tends be a hard adjustment for most. You will likely find that most people don't get up at the same time and rarely go to bed with any consistency. Changing this and developing rhythms isn't an easy process. It will be something the people in your Huddle struggle with. Undoubtedly, they will want to give up. And as the person discipling them, remember that you lay down your life to get them through this. If they can't get these rhythms down, our enemy will render them virtually ineffective because he has cut off their source of life and energy: the Father.

They will want to give up during this phase, so give them a tremendous amount of grace and keep reminding them why they are doing this. One helpful tidbit: many Huddle leaders find it helpful to text the people they're discipling each day, for 6 weeks straight, to remind them of the passage of scripture you're reading as a way of holding them accountable.

The same goes for taking a day off (Sabbath), an important weekly rhythm. You have to give a massive challenge and a massive invitation for them to make this happen in their life. They might fail more at this than they do in their daily rhythms. Many people are addicted to work, to emails, and to doing, doing, doing. It's so very difficult in our culture to take 24 whole hours off. You have to help people in your Huddle fight to take a Sabbath. The best way to do this is to model it in your own life. Invite them and their family to spend their day off with you and your family. Show them what it's like and why it's such a beautiful thing.

PHASE THREE: BOLDNESS IN MISSION

Very clearly, we are to be about our Father's business. We are the agents of the Kingdom. We have an interior world, but as we become deeply connected to the God of mission, we respond in kind since we have been made in the same image. We carry his authority and have been told to exercise his power. So every day, there is a mission.

A Huddle allows you to disciple your members in such a way that they integrate the mission into their way of seeing the world and balancing their relationships.

You can do this in two ways in a Huddle. First, use your Huddle time to get out on a mission together. Afterward, process the Kairos that was provoked.

You will notice that this is intricately worked into the framework we have laid out in this leader guide. Second, Huddle is about holding the people you're discipling accountable to living out the OUT component of Jesus' life through concrete, actionable plans. Every disciple is missional. It's part of the deal! Yet most of us simply don't live that way.

Now, when we first start interacting with this, some timidity is natural. More than likely we will stick to the People of Peace that we know well and in front of whom we won't risk embarrassing ourselves. *(See the Relational Mission chapter and the Octagon section from the appendix in Building a Discipling Culture for more details here.)*

But what happens when we sense we are supposed to pray for someone we don't know? Or ask someone we have only met once a personal question? Or ask for healing for someone we just passed on the street? Or maybe spend time in Section 8 government housing where people have to choose between buying food or paying rent? Or make a spiritual insight into the life of someone whom you know very well, even though you are scared what they may think of you afterward?

If you're like most people (including me when I was first starting out), the thought of this petrifies you! But we can't read scripture and avoid the fact that God prepares us to be present with others for a specific purpose. This third phase is an exercise in learning boldness and walking in the economy of a different kind of kingdom.

Does that mean you don't engage in a mission in the previous two phases? Of course not. It simply means that as someone learns the language, and as they have rhythms of listening to the Father regularly governing their lives, out of the overflow of this will be an increased intentionality, authority and boldness that wasn't present before. It starts from inside you and works its way out.

PHASE FOUR: LEADERSHIP

One of the stated expectations of a Huddle at the very beginning is that if you're in a Huddle, you will start one of your own someday or lead out a missional vehicle that will one day lead to the formation of leaders in a Huddle. This is how we keep the Gospel imperative of the Great Commission: *Make disciples who then make disciples who then make disciples.* A Huddle isn't just for our sake (though we receive great spiritual benefit from participating).

If we receive anything, it's so we can give it away. Once people know the agreed-on discipleship language, their lives are evidence of this. And when they have sustainable rhythms in their lives and begin to learn to boldly enter into mission, then the expectation is that they will begin a Huddle (or another missional/discipling endeavor) of their own. Every disciple leads someone, even if it's just 4 people.

TRUSTING
THE PROCESS

This guide lays out a helpful framework for you that is designed to allow you to find freedom within it. Now, here's an important caution: You will probably be tempted to evaluate the success or failure of your Huddle one Huddle gathering at a time. This is actually *very **unhelpful***.

Whenever we disciple people, there are ups and downs, and we can't evaluate it one snapshot at a time. We need a fuller, wider picture of what is happening. Often it's more helpful to look at 3-4 month chunks of time to see whether the trajectory is trending positively or negatively.

The process of Huddle is one the movement has used in every continent except Antarctica (still hoping to get there!) and in every cultural context imaginable. Trust the process! You've been in a Huddle, and you've seen transformation in your own life. Never forget that this framework is built for the journey you are on, as well as for the Huddle you lead.

CONTENT
AND CONTEXT

The discipling process is very much the convergence of Content and Context.

There are certain Content things we want the people we are investing in to know in the core of their being. It's the spiritual DNA that we are trying to pass on to them. At the same time, the Content is worthless if they don't know how to connect it to the Context of their lives. It's not just that we want people to know the Doctrine of the Trinity; we want that to change the way they live each and every day!

So we find that this meeting of Content (Word) and Context (Flesh) is actually all about Incarnation—the Word becoming Flesh. And what people have found is that the tools of LifeShapes are remarkably helpful in connecting Content and Context together. They aren't the end of the conversation; they are the beginning. It's that now we know how to use the scriptures well! They lead the Context of our lives more fully and more deeply into the scriptures.

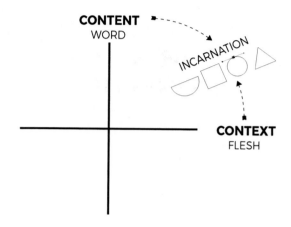

Jesus puts it this way: He says that a disciple is the wise man the Old Testament speaks about. That's who we want to be like. So in the closing parable on the Sermon on the Mount, he says the wise man is the one who HEARS the words of Jesus but is also the one who puts it into PRACTICE. The fool hears the words of Jesus, but doesn't do anything with it. Discipleship is shaping people to be wise people, able to hear and practice.

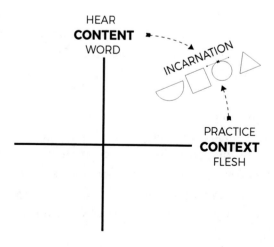

In reflecting on the Content that leaders are trying to impart to people, we see three elements:

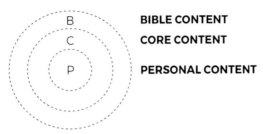

BIBLE CONTENT

CORE CONTENT

PERSONAL CONTENT

Everything is grounded in the BIBLE, then there is CORE content, and then there is PERSONAL content. Both core and personal content must find their root in the scriptures.

- **BIBLE CONTENT:** What do they need to know about the Bible? How can I best teach it? How will I teach them to read the scriptures well? How will all of this be simple, repeatable, and transferrable to the people they will be discipling? We highly recommend using the lens of Covenant and Kingdom for this. We have included this Bible content in the Year 1 framework you find in this guide

- **CORE CONTENT:** What are the key teachings or principles of Jesus, doctrine, or church values that need to work their way into the people you are leading? More than anything else, this Core content will become a language for them, and language creates culture. I have developed and the movement has refined LifeShapes to serve as a foundational language for this, but there are other particulars to your culture that you may want to develop alongside LifeShapes. Often there is language that your church has developed that you'll want here.

- **PERSONAL CONTENT:** Because discipleship is always a relational endeavor, you will be passing on your own spiritual

DNA to those you are investing in. But you want to be intentional with this rather than haphazard. What are the things in your faith that are central to your understanding that may not be as high on other people's radar? Maybe it's a specific kind of prayer you really latched onto. Maybe a way of seeing and interacting with the poor. Maybe it's the way you do hospitality and give people access to your life. You'll want to pass on these things that are specific to you.

In reflecting on the Context side of things, these three simple things can help you discern the Context of someone's life:

- **CHARACTER:** When I look at this person's life, where have I seen character growth? Where do I see character weaknesses? Where do the internal parts of their life need to look more like Jesus? What about the group as a whole? Remember, character is about BEING.

- **COMPETENCY:** When I look at this person's life, where have I seen competency growth? Where do I see competency weakness? What could Jesus do that they can't? What about the group as a whole? Remember, competency is about DOING.

- **SQUARE:** As you look at the LifeShape leadership square, where is this person? Are they still in D1? Have they hit the brick wall of D2 yet? Are they ready to receive more responsibility in D3? What about the group as a whole? If you can identify where the group and where individuals are on the Square, it helps you discern where to take the Huddle next.

The framework for this first year help you discern the Content and Context of your Huddle so you can lead your people forward.

The key to this is knowing at the outset what Core Content you want to pass onto them before you begin. Here is an exercise you can do to help you determine what the content is for you:

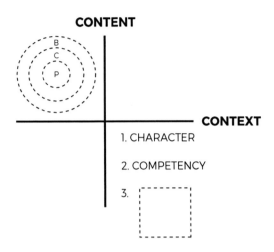

Fill in the Content you want to impart. This allows your Huddle to be contextualized to the leadership of both you and your wider church body:

BIBLE CONTENT:
· COVENANT + KINGDOM
·
·
·

CORE CONTENT:
· LIFESHAPES
·
·
·

PERSONAL CONTENT:
·
·
·

VALUE
OF THE TOOLS

As just discussed, LifeShapes help us connect the Content of the scriptures with the Context of someone's life. It's important to recognize that they also serve as a Picture, Mirror, and Window.

First, they serve as a Picture that helps us grasp and understand some of the most core principles of the Christian life.

Then, they serve as a Mirror, holding up the principles of scripture and the life of Jesus to our own life, allowing us to see ourselves. What do we like that we're seeing? What don't we like?

Lastly, they serve as a Window to help us see and understand the world. For instance, the more we understand the Semi-Circle and the principles of rest and work, the more we see life through that lens. It's simply how we see, interpret, and understand the world now.

HUDDLE IS NOT DISCIPLESHIP

Huddle is the ongoing, intentional, structured investment into leaders where they are learning to listen and respond to the voice of God. A leader invests his or her life into the lives of others, encouraging them to mine out their Kairos moments and map out plans for which they will be accountable.

However, the call to discipleship is an invitation into our lives, not just to a Huddle. It is both an organized and organic expression of relationship. The vehicle of Huddle is on the organized side of the spectrum; however, it is crucial for us to also do the organic things that are best described as access to our lives outside of Huddle.

DISCIPLESHIP IS...

ORGANIZED / STRUCTURED	**ORGANIC / SPONTANEOUS**
← – – – – – – – – – – – – –	– – – – – – – – – – – – →
HUDDLE	ACCESS TO LEADER'S LIFE

A commitment to discipling someone isn't just committing to the Huddle process. It's committing to inviting them into your life. It is access with boundaries, but access nonetheless. You cannot realistically expect to like the fruit you will get in investing in someone if the majority of the time they spend with you is Huddle. This is enormously important

CALIBRATING INVITATION AND CHALLENGE

Building a Discipling Culture discusses the importance of learning to calibrate invitation and challenge in every discipling relationship in Chapter 2. (I invite you to re-read it if you need to review.)

As you reflect on invitation and challenge, here are some helpful things to think through:

Communicate the culture of invitation and challenge on the front end

Make sure your participants know the nature of Huddle involves invitation and challenge. This will save you from blindsiding participants down the road and will also give you the language for future conversations if someone is struggling with being challenged. You can remind them that you are imitating the life and ministry of Jesus and that, for a discipling culture to take shape, we need to imitate Jesus. It's helpful to remind your participants that their willingness to receive invitation and challenge increases their capacity and integrity in delivering the same for their Huddles.

Remember that many leaders have not been discipled through the lens of invitation and challenge

In the current models of discipleship, most leaders are not introduced to this aspect. Remember, much of discipleship is better caught than taught, and therefore modeling invitation and challenge is absolutely imperative for a successful discipling relationship. How can they give what they have not received?

Find out which end of the continuum your leaders lean toward

All of us will naturally calibrate one better than the other. The goal is to help our participants identify which they lean toward and develop the skills of calibrating the other well. Calibrating both high invitation and high challenge is absolutely essential if we are to lead those we huddle into greater measures of Kingdom breakthrough.

You will inevitably have to calibrate challenge regarding logistical issues

The time will come when you find participants haven't followed through on their plan, don't show up, or aren't taking it seriously. Offering a gracious word of challenge in these moments will be important as this may stir a helpful Kairos.

- **For leaders prone to INVITATION:** Remind them of the gift they will be when they bring a needed word of challenge blanketed with the mercy they will naturally bring to the table.

It may be helpful to have them reflect on their story: How has God used challenge in their lives? For example, the sports coach or someone in their lives who wasn't willing to let them settle for status quo when they saw potential in them.

- **For leaders prone to CHALLENGE:** An axiom you may find helpful is "There is a difference between loving to speak the truth and speaking the truth in love." It is key for these leaders to have an opportunity to imitate the invitation calibrated by you. It's helpful to remember that "God's kindness leads you to repentance" (Romans 2:4).

BEFORE
YOUR HUDDLE BEGINS

- Make sure you've had a chance to participate in a Huddle before you begin leading your own. Don't assume that because you have led a small group in the past that you can easily lead a Huddle. They are vastly different. The best way to learn to lead a Huddle is to be in one first.

- The book *Building a Discipling Culture* is the foundational text for the Huddle. Make sure each participant has one before the Huddle begins.

- Really ask God who should be in your Huddle. Spend at least 3-4 weeks praying about this. The inclination will be to think strategically. That's fine—but don't let strategy interfere with who God wants to be in your Huddle. God will often surprise you with who he brings into the Huddle and who doesn't end up being part of it. Look for the People of Peace whom God has prepared for your Huddle. That's the person you want. Maybe write down the people who would be obvious choices first. Then, come back a week later and ask God to give you a few people who wouldn't be obvious choices.

- Make sure the people you are inviting into your Huddle are already leaders or know they are going to be expected to lead something in the future.

- More than likely, you will run into a few skeptical people when discussing Huddles. If they are massively cynical about Huddles and you find yourself trying to prove that a Huddle is of value, just pass on them for the time being. It's difficult to actively disciple someone who is cynical. There's a good chance that person will come around, but it will be the transformed lives of the other people in your Huddle that convince them. There are plenty of people who are looking for people to invest in them; find those people. Look for the People of Peace.

- When you invite someone into this relationship, don't invite him or her into your Huddle. That sounds like you are inviting them into a program. Invite them into a relationship where you will be investing in them, which will require organized time (Huddle) as well as more informal, organic time (access to your life).

- Make sure the people in your future Huddle know the enormous commitment level, specifically when it comes to keeping the Huddle time sacred on the calendar. You put a Huddle on the calendar, and then schedule the rest of your month. Obviously, you don't want to say it quite so forcefully, because they won't understand the importance of it from experience yet. Let them know it's OK to miss for unavoidable things, but being tired, busy, or stressed isn't a good reason to miss. They will always be at least one of those three things (if not a combination of them).

- Don't oversell yourself as the Huddle leader, especially if this is your first time leading a Huddle. Just as there is a learning curve for the people in your Huddle, there will be a learning curve for you. Make sure they know this will be a journey and a learning process, both for you and for them. They are learning how to be *discipled*, and you are learning to *disciple*. Remember the quote from G.K. Chesterton: "If it's worth doing, it's worth doing badly." Leading a Huddle is a skill you have to learn and develop like anything else in life. No one was born a great Huddle leader. You will be naturally more skilled at either invitation or challenge and will have to concentrate on improving the other. You have to put in time and effort and have patience. There will be times when you don't feel like you're doing well at leading your Huddle. That's normal! Pray more, stick with it, get coaching from a strong Huddle leader, and over time you will develop the skill set.

FREEDOM AND FRAMEWORK

The framework provided in this guide gives a foundational level of language, with a loose order, while equally trying to encourage you to discern the order for your group and the content you need to include that is not included in LifeShapes.

Essentially, we have broken the year into 10 five-week intervals. Each interval is simple and repeatable, and each builds on the previous weeks. Here is how each interval is structured.

THE FRAMEWORK

WEEK 1:	WEEK 2:	WEEK 3:	WEEK 4:	WEEK 5:
CONTENT TOOL	PERSONAL	LEADERSHIP	CHARACTER/ SKILL QUESTIONS	MISSION

- **Week 1: Content Tool.** Participants are introduced to a piece of content by reading about it ahead of time and then engaging in reflection and discussion.

- **Week 2: Personal.** The Huddle Leader teaches the tool from the previous week (in five minutes or less on a whiteboard, iPad, flip chart, etc). The participants are then asked to engage with the tool in the context of their own life on a personal level. By the end of the Huddle, each participant is able to clearly identify what God is saying to him or her and what he or she going to do about it.

- **Week 3: Leadership.** This time, a participant in the Huddle teaches the tool (in five minutes or less). The participants are then asked to engage with the tool in the context of either a group they are leading or the family they are helping lead. By the end of the Huddle, each participant is able to clearly identify what God is saying to him or her and what he or she is going to do about it.

- **Week 4: Character/Skills Questions.** Participants identify which question from a list of UP, IN, and OUT questions the Holy Spirit seems to be highlighting for them. They engage the process of discerning what God might be saying to them and what they are going to do about it.

- **Week 5: Mission.** Using the time normally allotted for Huddle, take the participants out on a short mission excursion. (A comprehensive list of ideas for this time is found in Part 3 of this guide.) At the end of the mission time together, process what God is saying and what they should do about it.

What you are doing is slowly introducing new pieces of language (the tools) and allowing them to engage with them on deeper and deeper levels, so that the tools move from being a Picture to a Mirror to a Window. What eventually happens is that their lives begin to embody the principles.

Coaching Tip: What happens when you can't get all the way around the Circle in one Huddle? You will find from time to time that people are having such a large Kairos that they need more time to observe, reflect, and discuss before they can articulate what God is saying. That's great! In that case, what God seems to be saying is that this is something he needs you to attend to in the next few weeks, and the plan is to continue to observe, reflect, and discuss outside of Huddle. In the next Huddle, check in again to see where the person is.

Moreover, the framework is simple, repeatable, and transferrable as they come to wrestle with starting their own Huddle. The pattern is just Tool, Personal, Leadership, Questions, Mission.

Remember: Regardless of what Content is inputted, at the end of each Huddle you want each participant to be able to articulate what God is saying to them and their plan for living into what God is saying.

In order, here are the 10 tools:

- Invitation + Challenge matrix: Culture of discipleship
- Learning Circle: Spiritual breakthrough
- Covenant and Kingdom triangles: Scripture defining reality
- Semi-Circle: Rhythm of Life
- Triangle: Deeper and balanced relationships
- Square: Multiplying discipling leaders
- Pentagon: Personal calling
- Hexagon: Prayer
- Heptagon: Communal spiritual health
- Octagon: Relational mission

THE FREEDOM

As we have already said multiple times, you should find freedom in the framework. You should to feel open and able to change up the order in which you go through these tools. Also, you may want to spend more time in one tool to ensure that the people you're discipling really are living it out. We have found this particularly true for the Semi-Circle, which addresses rhythms of life. Often, five Huddle gatherings aren't adequate time to see real breakthrough. Many Huddles concentrate on this for longer periods of time.

Furthermore, you may feel like the Holy Spirit is leading you toward a piece of Core content that isn't included in these 10 tools and that you need to veer towards that direction for a period of time. That's great! The good news is you can take your own content and put it through the framework we provide here.

The goal is for every Huddle leader to be able to discern where the Holy Spirit is taking the group and how God is actively shaping and forming the people within it.

Therefore, after several of the five- week intervals, there will be a simple exercise to help you discern the best place to go next.

CONTEXT: Evaluate the people in your group and the group as a whole

- Where are they on the Square right now?

- What Character weaknesses are there right now? Strengths?

- What Competency weaknesses are there right now? Strengths?

- Discern: Based on these questions and my reflections, I think God is saying my group needs to learn _____.

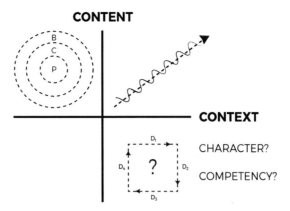

CONTENT: What Content fits what my group needs to learn next?

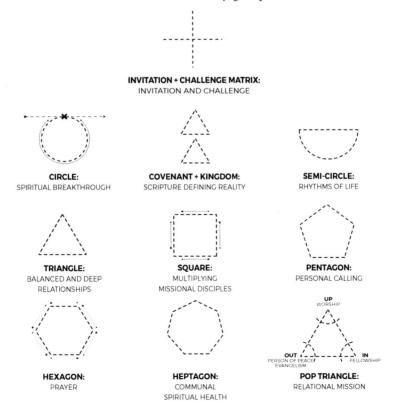

- Is there a LifeShape that would meet the Context need?

- Is there something specific they need to learn about the Bible that would meet the Context need?

- Is there something in my spiritual DNA that would meet the Context need?

- Is it something else?

For instance, let's say that through this discernment process you sense that, because so many in your group are going into difficult missional contexts, it will be important for them to have a strong hold on Doctrine. So you want to focus on Doctrine for a bit of time, specifically on the physical resurrection of Jesus. In order to give them something that is repeatable, simple, and transferrable, you do a five-week cycle that looks like:

WEEK 1:	WEEK 2:	WEEK 3:	WEEK 4:	WEEK 5:
CONTENT TOOL	PERSONAL	LEADERSHIP	CHARACTER/ SKILL QUESTIONS	MISSION
DOCTRINE: PHYSICAL RESURRECTION OF JESUS	WHAT IS GOD SAYING TO ME ABOUT HOW RESURRECTION AFFECTS MY LIFE?	WHAT IS GOD SAYING TO ME ABOUT HOW RESURRECTION AFFECTS HOW I LEAD?	STANDARD UP/IN/OUT QUESTIONS	DO A MISSION ACTIVITY THAT HAS INTRINSIC MEANING TO THE PHYSICAL RESURRECTION OF JESUS

Here are three examples:

- Take your Huddle to serve in a blood drive

- Pray for people who are sick to get well

- Meet a physical need within your close community

After completing this interval, do the same discernment exercise again. It is freedom within a framework. **This guide lists the framework in the order it most frequently occurs. But if necessary, feel free to step outside of this order, under the leading of the Holy Spirit.**

This interval framework does three very important things:

1. It allows a scriptural principle expressed in the tool to slowly incarnate itself into the life of someone, going from a Picture to a Mirror to a Window.

2. People regularly have to address the shape of their life through the UP/IN/OUT character and skills questions. By regularly and rhythmically facing these questions, we ensure that our lives take on the three dimensions of Jesus' life.

3. It creates a useful training environment for mission as the entire Huddle is regularly going OUT together, while also providing a place to process what they experience. Most people we know aren't terribly good at mission, and this is an important competency to learn.

Lastly, I strongly suggest not deviating from the framework for the first three intervals. The first three intervals (Invitation and Challenge, Spiritual Breakthrough, and Covenant and Kingdom) are foundational before going anywhere else with your Huddle.

For more detail on how the first year of a Huddle often transpires, please see Part 3 of *Building a Discipling Culture*.

> **Coaching Tip:** The participants in your Huddle need:
>
> -   The book *Building a Discipling Culture*
> -   The *Huddle Participant Guide* that accompanies this leader guide

INDIVIDUAL HUDDLE PATTERN

Every time you lead a Huddle, you are engaging with a simple, repeatable pattern. Half the reason Huddle is so transformational is because you enter into this process with each Huddle. You don't need to re-invent the wheel for each Huddle!

Here are the four key ingredients:

1. Review   2. Kairos   3.   4. 2Qs

REVIEW

Take 2-4 minutes for people to share how their plans went from the week before. At the end of every Huddle, the participants should be able to articulate, "This is what God is saying to me and this is what I'm going to do about it." Make make sure to hold them accountable to following through on their plans. You don't need to spend long doing it. Write down what their plans were, read them back the following Huddle, and simply ask if they did what they said they were going to do. In some Huddles you might want to hear how things went after following through, but the most important part is making sure they follow through. This is what spiritual partnership can look like.

KAIROS

Introduce a Kairos. Here are a few examples of what that can look like: (1) A mini-teaching with content you want them to wrestle with (never longer than 10 minutes). (2) Take them out on mission as a Huddle. Trust me—they will have a Kairos. (3) Have them read something ahead of time and bring their Kairos to Huddle. (4) Have them bring a Kairos from their own life to process. (5) Give a quick synopsis of the weekend teaching and have each person share his or her Kairos from it.

LEARNING CIRCLE

Take people through the Learning Circle, making sure you give time for people to observe, reflect, and discuss, as well as giving some of your own reflections using the discipleship tools you've learned (LifeShapes).

TWO QUESTIONS

At the conclusion of every Huddle, participants should be able to clearly articulate an answer to these two questions: What is God saying to you? What are you going to do about it?

SAMPLE HUDDLE OUTLINE

(Snacks and drinks are always a good idea)

7:00 People arrive and mingle

7:15 Pray and give the outline of night

7:18 Review (from your notes) each person's plan from the previous Huddle. Have each person say if he or she followed through or not.

7:20 Introduce Content (recap or mini-teaching)

7:30 Have everyone share his or her Kairos moments (write them down)

7:40 Engage in observation, reflection, and discussion

- You can go person by person

- You can deal with the big themes emerging

- You can hone in on one person and walk him or her around the Circle

8:10 Give each person a minute of silence and then have each person articulate what he or she believes God is saying to them. If they are wrestling with it still, give them some feedback and help them articulate the Kairos.

8:20 Give each person a minute of silence to process one thing they can do (their plan) to live into what they believe God is saying to them. Again, if they are struggling with a plan, give them a possible plan to help them. In each interval found in section 2 of this guide, you'll find a few suggestions of plans that would be helpful for each discipleship tool.

8:30 Give closing thoughts. Pray. Dismiss

PART 2

THE YEAR 1
FRAMEWORK

INTERVAL 1
INVITATION AND CHALLENGE

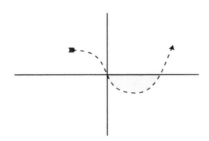

Helpful plans for invitation and challenge:

- Read one of the Gospels. How did Jesus calibrate invitation and challenge? And to what end?

- Find someone who is better at invitation or challenge than you. Watch them. Ask questions. What's their tone of voice? Body language? Phrases they use?

- Ask close friends/family. What do they see in you?

- Find one situation in the next week where you can demonstrate invitation and challenge

- Find one place in the past week where you didn't demonstrate invitation and challenge well.

WEEK 1
CONTENT TOOL

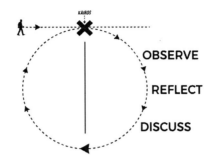

BEFORE HUDDLE

Have participants read chapters 1-2 of *Building a Discipling Culture*. Make sure they are ready to share what most grabbed their attention—this is code for their Kairos moment. Remember that they will probably be unfamiliar with this language at this point.

NOTES:

- The majority of this Huddle will be discussion oriented. Even though people in your Huddle may not know the language of the Learning Circle, you can take them around the first half of it by helping them observe, reflect, and discuss.

- Draw their attention to the Invitation + Challenge Matrix found in the Participant's Guide. This gives us a picture of the culture of discipleship, where we are being invited and challenged toward greater relationship and representation as children of the King.

- They will learn to calibrate invitation and challenge as they experience it in your Huddle.

- Remember to encourage your participants to read Covenant + Kingdom as the biblical, theological foundation for everything else they will learn in the Huddle.

WEEK 2
PERSONAL

BRIEF HUDDLE

1. Teach the Invitation and Challenge matrix in four minutes or less. Remember that in the following Huddle, one of them will be teaching it, so give them something they can imitate.

2. Allow them space to reflect on the teaching with maybe a minute of silence to allow them to identify their Kairos moment. (Again, remember that they don't have Kairos language yet.)

3. Using their thoughts from the last Huddle and the current Kairos, help them identify what God is saying to them and what they should do about it.

NOTES:

•   We're all naturally wired to feel more comfortable expressing invitation or challenge. How do we learn to calibrate both? Consider having them identify someone who calibrates well in the area in which they want to grow (i.e. body language, vocal tones, word choice, behaviors, attitudes). Suggest observing that person and how he or she expresses invitation or challenge and then seeking to incorporate those behaviors into their own lives.

•   Often we struggle to give others what we have not or cannot receive.

FOR THE NEXT HUDDLE:

Have them take time to put their life in each of the four Quadrants. Where are they seeing breakthrough in discipleship? Where are they cozy? Where is there apathy/death? Where are they discouraged and frustrated?

WEEK 3
LEADERSHIP

BRIEF HUDDLE OUTLINE:

1. Take two minutes and have everyone report out on whether they followed through on their plans. (See the coaching tip below.)

2. Have one of the participants teach the Invitation and Challenge matrix (in four minutes or less).

3. Have each participant plot out where either the group he or she is leading or his or her family is on the matrix. Allow them to reflect and discuss about their group/family, and you're your input into this discussion.

4. Get them to a place where they can clearly articulate what God is saying and one thing they can do to live into the Kingdom between now and your next Huddle, particularly in terms of what they are leading.

NOTES:

- Leaders define culture, so more often than not the culture of the group we lead will reflect the calibration of invitation and challenge in our leadership. Invitation without challenge will give us a cozy culture, while challenge without invitation will yield a discouraged culture.

- It's helpful to know that any group functioning in the cozy quadrant will have leaders functioning in the discouraged quadrant.

- Help them begin to think through what the journey of the Valley of the Shadow of Death might look like for the group/family they are leading.

Coaching Tip:

Holding people accountable to their plans

It's less important that that you hear how everything went in their plans than whether they followed through. Sometimes you might want to follow up and see what Kairos was produced from following through on the plan, but more importantly, you want to make sure they are following through. Beginning each Huddle by taking two minutes (no more than two!) to hold them accountable will prove helpful in them following through and building character. The easiest way to do this is for you to take notes each Huddle of what their plans are and then ask them the following Huddle if they did what they said they were going to do. (Have them answer yes or no.)

WEEK 4
CHARACTER / SKILLS
QUESTIONS

BRIEF HUDDLE OUTLINE:

1. Take two minutes and have each person report out if he or she followed through on his or her plan.

2. Give a 3-5 minute overview of the three-dimensional life that Jesus led and how we want to live that kind of life (no need to draw the Triangle out yet).

3. Have everyone identify his or her strongest and weakest dimension. Then, have everyone turn to the Character/Skills Questions on page 35 of the participant guide. Give them two minutes of silence to look at the character questions for their weakest dimension, allowing the Holy Spirit to identify one question for them to process.

4. Have each person share his or her question, and then engage in the process of observation, reflection, and discussion, helping each person identify.

IMPORTANT FOR NEXT HUDDLE:

The next Huddle will be going out on mission together. You might want to give some brief thoughts on that time and your expectations rather than surprising everyone.

WEEK 5
MISSION

THINGS TO CONSIDER:

- This can't be an optional week for anyone. You want everyone in the group to grow in this competency.

- Page 179 of this guide has a list of suggestions and ideas for what it can look like to do mission together as a Huddle.

- How prepared and competent are you in this missional endeavor?

- After doing mission, make sure the Huddle has time to process what God is saying.

INTERVAL 2
SPIRITUAL BREAKTHROUGH

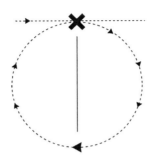

Helpful plans for spiritual breakthrough:

- Carry around a small notebook and write down every Kairos they have for the week

- Apply the Learning Circle as they read scripture

WEEK 1
CONTENT TOOL

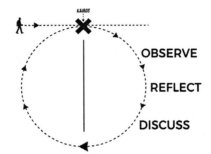

BEFORE HUDDLE

Have participants read the rest of Part 1 and the chapter on the Learning Circle in *Building a Discipling Culture*. Make sure they are ready to share what most grabbed their attention (this is code for their Kairos moment).

NOTES:

- The majority of this Huddle will be discussion oriented. Without them knowing the language of the Learning Circle, you can take them around the first half of it by helping them Observe, Reflect, and Discuss.

- Draw their attention to the parable of the wise and foolish man at the end of the Sermon on the Mount (Matthew 7:24-27). In what ways are they sometimes the wise man? In what ways are they sometimes the foolish man?

- We may solicit Kairos moments from a variety of sources, but the weekly rhythm of Huddle is identifying and processing a Kairos.

- During the discussion portion of the Circle that we get to introduce teaching, counsel, etc. in the Huddling process.

- We can only lead others as far around the Circle as they are prepared to go in that moment. Sometimes we need to give them space so God's spirit can continue to work in them.

- The Learning Circle empowers us to live a Covenant (Repentance / Right Relationship) and Kingdom (Believe / Representation) life.

ASSIGNMENT FOR NEXT HUDDLE

Have every participant bring three Kairos moments from now and the next meeting to the next Huddle.

WEEK 2
PERSONAL

BRIEF HUDDLE OUTLINE:

1. Teach the Learning Circle in four minutes or less. Remember that in the following Huddle, one of them will be teaching it, so give them something they can imitate.

2. Have each person share one Kairos moment that they brought to process. They don't need to share all three, just one.

3. Using their thoughts from the last Huddle and the current Kairos, help them identify what God is saying to them and what they should do about it by walking them around the Learning Circle.

NOTES:

- The biggest battle to win at the outset is to help people see that there are Kairos moments happening all around them. It's not as if they only happen once every couple of weeks.

- The effectiveness of the Learning Circle as a tool is largely dependent on our attention to each phase in the process around the Circle.

- Repentance answers the question, "What is God saying to me," and the Belief side of the Circle answers the question, "What will I do about it?"

- We cannot move to a Plan before we answer the question of what God is saying. Otherwise our Plan will sit on a faulty foundation. (Romans 10:17: "Faith comes from hearing the Word.")

- Make sure to remind them that you will start the next Huddle by asking them to share if they followed through on their plans. That's how the first two minutes of each Huddle will begin.

ASSIGNMENT FOR NEXT HUDDLE

Have each participant write down one Kairos from each day and bring the list to the next Huddle.

Coaching Tip:
How to help people who monopolize a lot of the group's time

One thing you get to do in Huddle is help people who struggle to get to the point of what they are experiencing learn how to get there quicker. If you have a group of people who struggle to articulate the most important things happening in their Kairos, adding a little time pressure is helpful, Tell people at the beginning of the group that each person will only get five minutes to go through Observe, Reflect, and Discuss portion of the Circle. To enforce this, use a timer. Do this for every person so that people realize no one is exempt. You'll be amazed how putting a little time pressure on people helps them focus to the most important elements.

WEEK 3
LEADERSHIP

BRIEF HUDDLE OUTLINE:

1. Take two minutes and have each person report out if he or she followed through on his or her plan.

2. Have one of the participants teach the Learning Circle in front of the group.

3. Pair people up. Have one partner share their Kairos, and get the other to walk him or her through the Learning Circle, making sure to articulate what God is saying to him/her and what he/she is going to do about. Then, have them switch and follow the same process.

4. Have 5-6 minutes of discussion about what they noticed as participants and as leaders.

5. Give affirmation and critique of what you observed.

NOTES:

*   Remember that you can solicit a Kairos by asking a question like, "What is most grabbing your attention this week?" or "What's really weighing on your heart this week?"

*   Help them observe by asking "what" questions.

- Help them reflect by asking "why" and "how" questions, or questions like, "Where does the rubber hit the road for you one this?"

- Help them discuss by sharing your own thoughts about their observations and reflections.

- Ultimately, you are trying to help them hear what the Lord is saying to them.

- Once they have identified something from the Lord, ask them how they might respond. What is the plan?

Coaching Tip:

It's never too early to point out that Huddle is both an investment into them and also a training vehicle. You are already training them to lead Huddle by leading one of their fellow participants through the Learning Circle.

WEEK 4
CHARACTER / SKILLS
QUESTIONS

BRIEF HUDDLE OUTLINE:

1. Take two minutes and have each person report out if he or she followed through on his or her plans.

2. Give a quick overview about the three-dimensional life that Jesus led and how we want to live that kind of life.

3. Have everyone identify their weakest dimension from the Huddle they last discussed Character/Skills. Then, have everyone turn to the Character/Skills Questions on page 35 of the Participant's Guide. Give them two minutes of silence to look at the Skills questions for their weakest dimension, allowing the Holy Spirit to identify one question for them to process.

4. Have each person share his or her question. Then engage in the process of reflection and discussion, helping each person identify what God is saying and what they are going to do about it.

Coaching Tip:
What if someone doesn't follow through on his or her plan?
Simply ask them "Why?" They might have a very good reason, or they might not. The answer to this question will allow you to calibrate invitation and challenge. Don't make assumptions. Try to find out what's really going on.

IMPORTANT FOR NEXT HUDDLE

The next Huddle will be going out on mission together. You might want to give some brief thoughts on that time and your expectations rather than surprising everyone.

WEEK 5
MISSION

THINGS TO CONSIDER:

- This can't be an optional week for anyone. You want everyone in the group to be growing in this competency.

- Page 179 of this guide has a list of suggestions and ideas for what it can look like to do mission together as a Huddle.

- How prepared and competent are you in this missional endeavor?

- After doing mission, make sure the Huddle has time to process what God is saying.

Coaching Tip:
Is most of your time spent in Huddle?

DISCIPLESHIP IS...

ORGANIZED /
STRUCTURED

ORGANIC /
SPONTANEOUS

◄ - ►

HUDDLE

ACCESS TO YOUR LIFE

Investing in someone's life has both an Organized and an Organic context. This section of the Leader Guide is mostly about the organized side of things in the Huddle.

An important question to be asking two intervals in is this: How much time do the people you're investing in get with you outside of Huddle? They need to see your life so they can see what these principles look like in the life of someone else. You don't need to be a perfect example, but they do need a living one. The key is to invite them into things you are already doing.

Here are some easy things to do that will give your Huddle participants access to your life:

- Invite them over to dinner with you and your family (invite more than one of them with your families as well).

- If you have to run to the grocery store, have them come with you and have them share what the Lord has been doing in their life as you shop.

- Have them come to the movies with you

- Do you need a ride to the airport? See if one of them can drive you.

- Have them go to a baseball or soccer game you're attending that your kids are in.

Again, you don't have to set up times that are "special" for them to process with you. Simply invite them into the things you're already doing!

INTERVAL 3
SCRIPTURE DEFINING REALITY

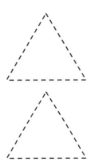

Helpful plans for covenant and kingdom:

- If someone is struggling with Identity, have him or her read Romans 8 once a day and record the Kairos he or she has each time he or she reads it.

- Have people reflect on their relationship with the Father. Read about the Baptism of Jesus in Mark 1. How does this hit you?

- Read the Gospels. Every time the Father says something to the Son, the Father is also saying it to you, because Paul tells us that when the Father sees us, he now sees Jesus. Do you see the Father saying those things to you?

WEEK 1
CONTENT TOOL

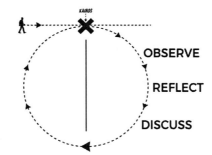

BEFORE HUDDLE

Have participants read the Covenant and Kingdom explanation in their participant guide on page 39. It is also included in this guide on page 185. If they desire to read more about this, have them pick up a copy of *Covenant and Kingdom: The DNA of the Bible.*

NOTES:

- The majority of this Huddle will be discussion-oriented. Take them around the Repent half of the Learning Circle by helping them to Observe, Reflect, and Discuss.

- Come to the Huddle with 3-4 different passages of scripture. Read one and then discuss it by having people identify what is going on. For instance, you could read select passages from Hosea 1 and 2 and discuss how this is a Covenantal passage where God is the spurned lover but longs to forgive and go back to the beginning and see Israel in a new light, giving her a new identity. Give the Huddle a few passages so they can see how these themes weave throughout scripture.

- Have them randomly pick a passage and read it, and help them see the themes woven within with the lens of Covenant and Kingdom.

Coaching Tip:
Here are a couple of examples from scripture that you can use:

1) Hosea 1-2
2) Jonah
3) Story of Joseph
4) Psalm 88

ASSIGNMENT FOR NEXT HUDDLE:

Have everyone in the Huddle read the same passages of scripture each day. We recommend using the Daily Moravian Prayer text, as these are the readings I do every day. For each New Testament reading, have them write down which of the six words the reading was speaking most specifically to (Covenant: Father, Identity, Obedience; or Kingdom: King, Authority, Power) and what their Kairos was from the reading.

WEEK 2
PERSONAL

BRIEF HUDDLE OUTLINE:

1. Did everyone bring their assignment from reading the scriptures each day? Ask for a yes or no answers to hold them accountable.

2. Teach the Covenant and Kingdom triangles in four minutes or less. Remember that in the following Huddle, one of them will be teaching it, so give them something they can imitate.

3. Have each person share a Kairos he or she would like to process from their exercise.

4. Walk through the full Learning Circle.

5. At the conclusion, each person should be able to articulate what God is saying and one thing they can do to live into it based on the Kairos provoked from the Covenant and Kingdom triangles

NOTES:

- When being exposed to this for the first time, most people see the theme of Identity come up pretty quickly. Make sure you have a few plans ahead of time that might be able to suggest knowing this theme will probably surface.

- The discussion part of the Huddle is a place where you can give some personal stories and testimonies of how Identity has been the key to many of the things in your life. (Some frequent themes: You don't have to earn love, you don't have to earn favor, authority is based on your secure identity, etc.)

Coaching Tip:

It's good to have the Learning Circle visible in front of the group so that they continually see the process in which they are engaging.

WEEK 3
LEADERSHIP

BRIEF HUDDLE OUTLINE:

1. Take two minutes and have each person report out if he or she followed through on his or her plan.

2. Have one of the participants teach the Covenant and Kingdom triangles.

3. Ask the group to evaluate what they are leading (group they are leading or family): What is the group stronger in—Covenant or Kingdom? Why are they stronger? Why are they weaker in the other? What does this reveal about their leadership? Does this in any way connect to their personal Kairos from the previous Huddle?

4. Take the Kairos you've provoked around the Learning Circle so that everyone is able to articulate what God is saying to create a plan.

KINGDOM PERSPECTIVE

We need to see failure not as a roadblock but as a steppingstone that leads toward more Kingdom breakthrough.

NOTES:

- Again, identity will probably be central to this conversation. You may find that the people they are leading are poor at Covenant because they are trying to earn something by doing Kingdom things or that they are doing little for the Kingdom because they feel they don't have the authority needed to do what is necessary.

Coaching Tip:

What if people are overreaching on their plans?

Often it is helpful to let people make bigger plans than they can achieve and use the Kairos of the failure lead them toward a greater issue going on in their life that the Lord is dealing with. Because you are holding them accountable to their plans, you know that any failure will be attended to and help them understand that it's all part of the process.

WEEK 4
CHARACTER / SKILLS QUESTIONS

HUDDLE OUTLINE:

1. Take two minutes and have each person report out if he or she followed through on his or her plan from the previous Huddle.

2. Give a one-minute review about the three-dimensional life that Jesus led and how we want to live that kind of life. (Remember that one of the future intervals will go into far more depth about this.)

3. Have everyone identify their strongest dimension in their personal life right now. Give them two minutes to review the questions in their strongest area, asking the Holy Spirit to reveal a positive aspect that they are doing well in that area through the question that's coming to the surface.

4. Have each person share his or her question and why the Holy Spirit is affirming something good in him or her. Then engage in the process of reflection and discussion, helping each person identify what God is saying and what he or she is going to do about it.

Coaching Tip:
The value of processing a positive Kairos moment is positive reinforcement. We value what we celebrate!

NOTES:

- **It is important for the Huddle participants to see that many of our Kairos moments are positive and that God is inviting us even further into the Kingdom through that affirmation.**

- If the positive affirmation that stood out was "Do I pursue intimacy with Jesus?" and we are sensing a strong "YES!" in our

Response, it is a gift to us! We not only have the desire to spend time with Jesus, but we are doing it! What else might God want to give us? What other ways might we pursue intimacy with Jesus?

IMPORTANT FOR NEXT HUDDLE

The next Huddle will be going out on mission together. You might want to give some brief thoughts on that time and your expectations rather than surprising everyone.

WEEK 5
MISSION

THINGS TO CONSIDER:

- This can't be an optional week for anyone. You want everyone in the group to be growing in this competency.

- Page 179 of this guide has a list of suggestions and ideas for what it can look like to do mission together as a Huddle.

- Either at the start of the Huddle or at the end, read a story from the Bible with a similar mission experience and then tie it back to the Covenant and Kingdom triangles to take the tool even further.

- How prepared and competent are you in this missional endeavor?

- After doing mission, make sure the Huddle has time to process what God is saying

DISCERNMENT EXERCISE

WHERE SHOULD THE HUDDLE GO NEXT?

CONTEXT: Evaluate the people in your group and the group as a whole

- Where are they on the Square right now?

  _____
  _____
  _____

- What Character weaknesses are there right now? Strengths?

  _____
  _____
  _____

- What Competency weaknesses are there right now? Strengths?

  _____
  _____
  _____

- Discern: Based on these questions and my reflections, I think God is saying my group needs to learn

  _____
  _____
  _____

CONTENT: What Content fits what my group needs to learn next?

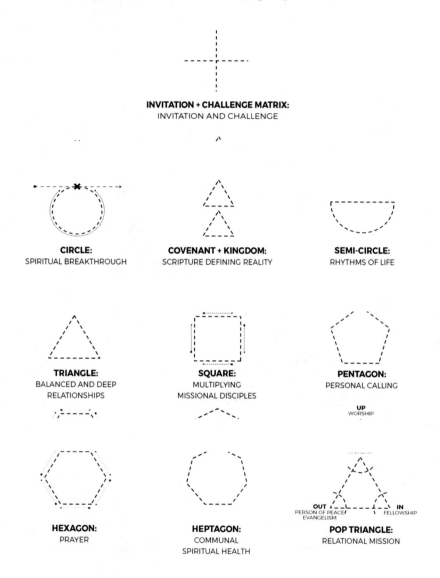

INVITATION + CHALLENGE MATRIX:
INVITATION AND CHALLENGE

CIRCLE:
SPIRITUAL BREAKTHROUGH

COVENANT + KINGDOM:
SCRIPTURE DEFINING REALITY

SEMI-CIRCLE:
RHYTHMS OF LIFE

TRIANGLE:
BALANCED AND DEEP
RELATIONSHIPS

SQUARE:
MULTIPLYING
MISSIONAL DISCIPLES

PENTAGON:
PERSONAL CALLING

UP
WORSHIP

HEXAGON:
PRAYER

HEPTAGON:
COMMUNAL
SPIRITUAL HEALTH

OUT
PERSON OF PEACE/
EVANGELISM

IN
FELLOWSHIP

POP TRIANGLE:
RELATIONAL MISSION

- Is there a LifeShape that would meet the Context need?

- Is there something specific they need to learn about the Bible that would meet the Context need?

- Is there something in my spiritual DNA that would meet the Context need?

- Is it something else?

I'm discerning that the next Content tool is:

_____

_____

_____

_____

_____

_____

_____

CONTENT

B
C
P

CONTEXT

1. CHARACTER

2. COMPETENCY

3.

INTERVAL 4
RHYTHMS OF LIFE

IMPORTANT NOTE: Many Huddle leaders need to spend more than one five-week interval on the principles of rest and work. This may be an interval where you spend an extended amount of time on because it is so difficult for people to embrace this way of living. They've been programmed to do life in the exact opposite way!

Helpful plans for rhythms of life:

- Have them turn off all electronic devices for 24 hours during their Sabbath day.

- Daily scripture reading text. Have each member of the Huddle text which passage of scripture they read that day, what God said, and what they are going to do about it.

- Take a one-week period and track how every hour is spent. How are you investing time, energy and resources? It's all about intentionality.

- How intentional are you?

- Are you aware of the return you are looking for?

- What's the connection between the first two questions?

WEEK 1
CONTENT TOOL

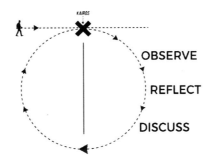

BEFORE HUDDLE

Have participants read the chapter on the Semi-Circle in *Building a Discipling Culture*. Make sure they are ready to share what most grabbed their attention and served as their Kairos.

NOTES:

The majority of this Huddle will be discussion-oriented. At this point, you don't want to get to the "What is God saying to me?" part of the discussion. That will come next week. Instead, you can take them around the first half of the Learning Circle by helping them Observe, Reflect, and Discuss.

- Know going into this interval on Rhythms of Life how poor most people are at living out the principle at working from a place of rest. It will be very important for you to live out this principle so you can give your life as an example of what this can look like.

ASSIGNMENT FOR NEXT HUDDLE

- Take a one-week period and track how every hour is spent. How are you investing time, energy and resources? It's all about intentionality.
  - How intentional are you?
  - Are you aware of the return you are looking for?
  - What's the connection between the first two questions?

WEEK 2
PERSONAL

BRIEF HUDDLE OUTLINE:

1. Teach the Semi-Circle in four minutes or less. Remember that in the following Huddle, one of them will be teaching it, so give them something they can imitate.

2. Allow them space to reflect on the teaching with a minute of silence to try to identify their Kairos moment.

3. Using their thoughts from the last Huddle and the current Kairos, help them identify what God is saying to them and what they should do about it.

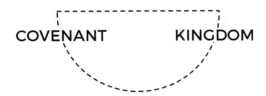

COVENANT   KINGDOM

NOTES:

- The Semi-Circle gives us permission for rest and accountability for abiding.

- It is difficult to abide spiritually when you are not rested physically. (How many times have you fallen asleep while praying?) The reverse is also difficult: It is difficult to rest physically when you are anxious emotionally/spiritually.

- Remember, rest is not simply defined as "time alone with Jesus." It is also time with close member in the Body of Christ who, when we spend time with them, gives us energy and life and makes us feel closer to the Father.

- Another helpful way of understanding rest is the word "re-creation." What re-creates you?

WEEK 3
LEADERSHIP

BRIEF HUDDLE OUTLINE:

1. Take two minutes and have each person report out if he or she followed through on his or her plans.

2. Have one of the participants teach the Semi-Circle.

3. Have each participant plot out where they believe the group (or family) he or she is leading currently on the pendulum. If they are Abiding, what does that look like? If they are in a fruitful season, what does that look like? If they are being pruned, how are they making the most of that season?

4. Get them to a place where they can clearly articulate what God is saying and one thing having to do with what they are leading that they can do to live into the Kingdom between now and your next Huddle.

NOTES:

- Being able to identify where the group you are leading is on the Semi-Circle is an incredibly helpful analytical tool that Jesus gives us in John 15. It shows us how to make the most of where we are and what is just around the corner. It can help decompress the anxiety and fear of the unknown.

- Know that pruning is always painful for people, particularly for those who have never understood this was the process they were going through. How can you help them through that process if they are there?

- People often use the phrase "It feels like I'm pushing a boulder up a hill" to describe what is often an indicator of what it can feel like for a group when they are being pulled back to a time of pruning and abiding. However, it could also be that they need to persevere and continue pushing for breakthrough.

WEEK 4
CHARACTER / SKILLS
QUESTIONS

BRIEF HUDDLE OUTLINE:

1. Take two minutes and have each person report out if he or she followed through on his or her plan.

2. Have everyone turn to the Character questions for the OUT dimension.

3. Give them two minutes of silence in looking at the Character OUT questions, allowing the Holy Spirit to identify one question for them to process.

4. Have each person share his or her question and then engage in the process of reflection and discussion.

5. Have the group discern together what they feel, collectively, God is saying to the Huddle as a whole when it comes to OUT.

6. The plan: Based on what God is saying to the Huddle, have the group craft the plan together specifically for what next Huddle's missional endeavor looks like.

IMPORTANT FOR NEXT HUDDLE

The next Huddle will be going out on mission together based on the plan the group creates in this Huddle. Make sure you iron out the details for what that means for the upcoming Huddle.

WEEK 5
MISSION

THINGS TO CONSIDER:

- This can't be an optional week for anyone. You want everyone in the group to be growing in this competency.

- This should be a particularly exciting week because your Huddle crafted the OUT you're going to do together.

- How prepared and competent are you in this missional endeavor?

- After doing mission, make sure the Huddle has time to process what God is saying.

INTERVAL 5
BALANCED AND DEEP RELATIONSHIPS

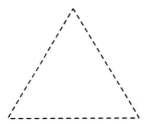

Helpful plans for balanced and deep relationships:

- Sit down with your spouse every Sunday night for six weeks and, using the Triangle and UP/IN/OUT, plot out what your week looks like. If it is out of balance, shift something around! Use the Triangle to order and prioritize your schedule.

- Read through the Gospel of Mark and identify where Jesus is doing UP/IN/OUT

WEEK 1
CONTENT TOOL

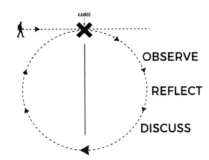

BEFORE HUDDLE

Have participants read the chapter on the Triangle in *Building a Discipling Culture*. Make sure they are ready to share what most grabbed their attention and served as their Kairos.

NOTES:

The majority of this Huddle will be discussion-oriented. At this point, you don't want to get to the "What is God saying to me?" part of the discussion. That will come next week. Instead, take the group around the first half of the Learning Cirlce, helping them to Observe, Reflect, and Discuss.

Coaching Tip:

The inclination with the Triangle is to increase activity. However, it is more about paying attention to where Jesus is already at work and being more intentional in what you are already doing.

WEEK 2
PERSONAL

BRIEF HUDDLE OUTLINE:

1. Teach the Triangle in three minutes or less. Remember that in the following Huddle, one of them will be teaching it, so give them something they can imitate.

2. Have them score themselves, on a scale of 1–10, for UP/IN/OUT. Have them share their scores and give a little context to them.

3. Allow them space to reflect on what they just shared with maybe a minute of silence to try to identify their Kairos moment.

4. Using their thoughts from the last Huddle and the current Kairos, help them identify what God is saying to them and what they should do about it.

NOTES:

- The Triangle is probably the most familiar of the principles we are trying to pass onto them. As such, you'll need to be careful to not glaze over the principles but instead make sure that each dimension of Jesus' life is held up to their life as a mirror.

WEEK 3
LEADERSHIP

BRIEF HUDDLE OUTLINE:

1. Take two minutes and have each person report out on whether he or she followed through on his or her plan.

2. Have one of the participants teach the Triangle in three minutes or less.

3. Have them score what they are leading (group or family) on a scale of 1–10 for UP/IN/OUT. Have them share their scores and give a little context to them. Make sure that in the discussion you point out that everything we lead needs to be three-dimensional in all it does.

4. Allow them space to reflect on what they just shared with maybe a minute of silence so they can try to identify their Kairos moment.

5. Using their thoughts from the last Huddle and the current Kairos, help them identify what God is saying to them and what they should do about it.

Coaching Tip:

Leaders define culture, so if we want to see our people grow in the UP, IN or OUT dimension, we must be prepared to lead that way. In what ways are the things we are leading a reflection of us?

WEEK 4
CHARACTER / SKILLS QUESTIONS

BRIEF HUDDLE OUTLINE:

1. Take two minutes and have each person report out on whether he or she followed through on his or her plan.

2. Have everyone turn to the Character/Skills questions. Based on their weakest area from the previous Huddle, have them read through the Skills question of that dimension.

3. What is a question that they need to be asking of their group that isn't listed?

4. Have each person share his or her question, and then engage in the process of reflection and discussion. Why did this question come to mind?

5. Using the Learning Circle, have each person identify what God is saying and what he or she is going to do about it.

The questions we've written aren't all the questions we could be asking of the groups we are leading. What is a question that God might be asking of our group that isn't listed?

IMPORTANT FOR NEXT HUDDLE

The next Huddle will be going out on mission together. You might want to give some brief thoughts on that time and your expectations rather than surprising everyone.

Coaching Tip:

Have a few of your participants walk each other around the Learning Circle in Point 5 so that they have a chance to practice being a Huddle leader in a safe environment. They don't all need to do this, but do so with a few people, giving them some affirmation and critique.

WEEK 5
MISSION

THINGS TO CONSIDER:

- This can't be an optional week for anyone. You want everyone in the group to be growing in this competency.

- Pick something missional to do as a Huddle that will be an easy win for those you are investing in. With all the focus on OUT in the last 6 weeks, make sure they get a win they can feel good about.

- After doing mission, make sure the Huddle has time to process what God is saying.

INTERVAL 6
BALANCED AND DEEP RELATIONSHIPS

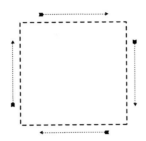

Helpful plans for multiplying missional disciples:

- Read through one of the Gospels and point out the different places Jesus demonstrates the different kinds of leadership. How is he calibrating invitation and challenge for each?

- Identify the times they've learned to do something and how that took the path of the Square.

- Identify the times where they've hit the wall at D2 and went back to find a new D1 vision.

- Identify where they've been launched into D3, skipping D1 and D2. What happened?

WEEK 1
CONTENT TOOL

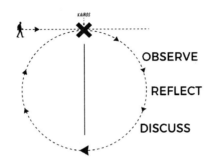

BEFORE HUDDLE

Have participants read the chapter on the Square in *Building a Discipling Culture*. Make sure they are ready to share what most grabbed their attention and served as their Kairos.

NOTES:

- The majority of this Huddle will be Discussion-oriented. At this point, you don't want to get to the "What is God saying to me?" part of the discussion. That will come next week. You can take them around the first half of the Learning Circle, helping them to Observer, Reflect, and Discuss together.

- The Square is the vision for Huddles. Huddle is the process of reproducing what we have received from others.

- In D2 we're tempted to find a new vision to escape the pain and discomfort of dying to self or to quit the journey all together.

- There are no shortcuts or fast tracks through D2. Under the pressure of D2, we discover our true character.

- WARNING: Do not let your gift take you where your character cannot sustain you. The devil loves to elevate gifting without character. He knows the higher he takes you the further you (and the others with you) fall.

Coaching Tip:

When we are squeezed, we see what something is made of. With an orange, we expect orange juice. With an apple, we expect apple juice. And when a Christian is squeezed, we expect to get Jesus. In D2, we are squeezed and often we get things that look more like us and not Jesus.

WEEK 2
PERSONAL

BRIEF HUDDLE OUTLINE:

1. Teach the Square in four minutes or less. Remember that in the following Huddle, one of them will be teaching it, so give them something they can imitate.

2. Allow them space to reflect on what they just heard with maybe a minute of silence to try to identify their Kairos moment.

3. Using their thoughts from the last Huddle and the current Kairos, help them identify what God is saying to them and what they should do about it using the Learning Circle.

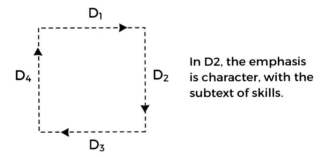

In D2, the emphasis is character, with the subtext of skills.

In D3, the emphasis is skills, with the subtext of character."

NOTES:

- It is very difficult to advance through each of the discipling phases (D1-D4) without receiving the appropriate leadership (L1- L4).

- The discipline of taking Kairos moments around the Circle is what keeps us moving around the Square.

- D2 usually takes the longest of the four phases, because this is the laying of the foundation for any new thing we're learning.

- Consider how farming a crop illustrates each of the four phases. Consider how children go through the four phases on their journey to adulthood.

WEEK 3
LEADERSHIP

BRIEF HUDDLE OUTLINE:

1. Take two minutes and have each person report out on whether he or she followed through on his or her plan.

2. Have them partner up in pairs.

3. Using the Square to reflect on the four styles of Leadership (L1-L4), have them reflect on which styles are they most comfortable with in the group/family they are leading. Are they a visionary leader? Do they enjoy walking with others in the midst of their darkest times? Do they enjoy the process of coaching, pushing others out of the nest? Can they delegate and release others into responsibility?

4. What style of leadership are they weakest in? Have them give examples of what their strength and weakness currently looks like.

5. Have each person walk his or her partner through the Learning Circle, helping him or her to identify what God is saying to them and what they should do about it using the Learning Circle. Give affirmation and critique.

6. Point out that in doing this, they are engaging in D3/L3.

7. Have someone volunteer to lead *the next whole Huddle*, which

will be on the Character/Skills questions. Tell the volunteer that he or she will do what he or she has seen you do several times.

8.   Point out that this is you actively walking them around the Square in real time.

NOTES:

- As leaders we are often guilty of treating our leaders as though they are in D4, expecting them to do for others what we have yet to do for them.

- We are also tempted to share compelling vision from up front and then release leaders into D3 responsibility without giving them the opportunity to pass through the phase "I do, you help."

- We are often guilty of seeking "plug and play" leaders who can "do" the ministry without giving consideration to what those leaders need by way of personal investment.

- Our trophies should be the leaders we raise up and send out, not those hired for what they've already accomplished.

- Our willingness to lead others through D2 (even our leaders) will yield a discipling culture and build a foundation for building eternal significance.

IMPORTANT FOR NEXT HUDDLE

Make sure you give clear instructions to the person leading your next Huddle, giving him or her a chance to ask questions. Remind the volunteer that while he or she is leading, you will still help. Give the volunteer the outline of the next Huddle (see following page).

Coaching Tip:

Our trophies should be the leaders we raise up and send out, not those hired for what they've already accomplished.

WEEK 4
CHARACTER / SKILLS
QUESTIONS

IMPORTANT HUDDLE NOTE:

Remember, you are serving primarily as a coach for the participant leading this Huddle. Your main responsibility is to listen, observe, and give feedback at the end of Huddle.

BRIEF HUDDLE OUTLINE FOR YOUR HUDDLE LEADER:

1. Introduce Huddle leader for the day. Pray for him or her and let him or her lead!

2. Take two minutes and have each person report out if he or she followed through on his or her plan.

3. Have everyone identify his or her strongest and weakest dimension currently. Then, have everyone turn to the Character/ Skills Questions in their participant guide on page 35. Give them two minutes of silence to look at the Character questions for their weakest dimension, allowing the Holy Spirit to identify one question for them to process.

4. Have each person share his or her question and then engage in the process of reflection and discussion, helping each person identify what God is saying and what he or she is going to do about it.

5. Have everyone engage in affirmation and critique of the person leading the Huddle, with you leading the way. Remember that when you are first doing this, it is helpful to use a 3:1 ratio of three affirmations for every one critique.

Notes:

- Do your best not to step in and save the person if he or she gets in trouble. You are allowing him or her a chance to make mistakes but to do so in a safe environment.

- Take notes as they are leading for you to reference during the time of affirmation and critique.

- Over-praise and over-celebrate them. Remember, what you value you celebrate, and what you celebrate you value!

- Once the Huddle is over, give a few closing thoughts on how to understand the Square based on their experience of this Huddle.

IMPORTANT FOR NEXT HUDDLE

The next Huddle will be out at a restaurant somewhere where the group won't engage in mission intentionally but will just enjoy each other and take a break. Give them the details for this gathering.

WEEK 5
MISSION

BRIEF OUTLINE OF HUDDLE:

- Meet at a restaurant and just enjoy each other over a meal and good conversation.

- Have people share some of their favorite stories from the past few months and some of the things they've learned.

- Have people share the growth they've seen in others.

WHY HUDDLES
PLATEAU AND STALL

1) THE PEOPLE IN YOUR HUDDLE AREN'T LEADING ANYTHING.

This is probably the No. 1 reason Huddles plateau and stall. It makes complete sense. For many people, discipleship is equated with "understanding the Bible better" or something akin to "inner transformation." Both are key aspects of discipleship, but certainly not the only ones to which we should be attending. Perhaps one of the largest components of the life of a disciple is going out and making disciples and *leading people out* in Kingdom mission. That makes the Huddle a much more dynamic environment, because the people you're investing in are experiencing success, failure, frustration, breakthrough, etc. in any given week. We often forget that Jesus deployed his disciples early in the game, but they were still connected to him. So in Mark 9, we see the disciples unable to cast out a demon. They come back to Jesus and ask why. "Oh... well for that one it requires prayer and fasting." (We can almost picture Jesus shrugging his shoulders as he answers.) The best discipling environments mean you have people that are out there doing the work of the Kingdom.

2) YOUR HUDDLE HAS NO DIRECTION.

There are two questions you want to be constantly asking as you're praying and preparing for your upcoming Huddle. First, what is God doing in your group in this current season of development? Second, what does he want to attend to in this specific Huddle? Sure, there is a loose framework that we've provided for the first year of Huddle with the LifeShapes, but that's just a framework. In other words, when it feels like your Huddle is drifting and you're uncertain what God wants to do with the people he's given you to invest in, people pick up on this, and it can become aimless and listless. Ask the Lord to give you clarity and direction on what he's trying to attend to with the people in your Huddle.

3) YOU'RE NOT CALIBRATING INVITATION AND CHALLENGE WELL.

Jesus was able to invite his disciples into relationship with him while also challenging them to live into their Kingdom responsibility. He did both. They got full access to his life and more time than anyone else by a country mile… but they also were challenged about the places in their life that were living outside of the ways of the Kingdom. Every leader is better at one than the other. Huddles can plateau when a leader is creating a culture that doesn't have a full expression of both. If you're all challenge, people will get frustrated and discouraged and never truly believe you care about them. If you're all invitation, people will only ever want to hang out and do fun, comfortable things they are good at and rarely push into the difficult things to which Jesus calls us. A Huddle has to have both.

4) HUDDLE IS THE ONLY CONTEXT FOR YOUR INVESTMENT IN THEIR LIFE.

This is a classic mistake people make in their first Huddle. They treat it much like the other discipleship vehicles they've used before and misunderstand that for true discipleship to happen, you need both the ORGANIZED and the ORGANIC. Huddle is the organized discipleship vehicle that has a regular and rhythmic pattern that is focused on discipleship and investment. However, we also need an organic component. People need access to your life outside of the Huddle. Invariably, people forget the more organic component and compartmentalize discipleship to the 90 minutes spent together in Huddle.

These few people you're investing in need more. Fold them into the things you're already doing in life and let them watch. If you're having dinner, invite them and their families over for dinner. If they are hitting a brick wall of some sort and you have to get to the airport, have them drive you and talk about it on the ride. If you like the movies, go to the movies with them. Remember, if you have a good life already, you just have to share that with them!

DISCERNMENT EXERCISE

WHERE SHOULD THE HUDDLE GO NEXT?

CONTEXT: Evaluate the people in your group and the group as a whole

- Where are they on the Square right now?

  _____

  _____

  _____

- What Character weaknesses are there right now? Strengths?

  _____

  _____

  _____

- What Competency weaknesses are there right now? Strengths?

  _____

  _____

  _____

- Discern: Based on these questions and my reflections, I think God is saying my group needs to learn

  _____

  _____

  _____

CONTENT: What Content fits what my group needs to learn next?

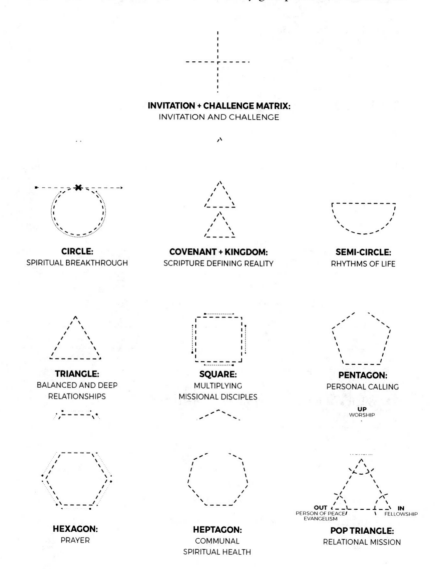

INVITATION + CHALLENGE MATRIX:
INVITATION AND CHALLENGE

CIRCLE:
SPIRITUAL BREAKTHROUGH

COVENANT + KINGDOM:
SCRIPTURE DEFINING REALITY

SEMI-CIRCLE:
RHYTHMS OF LIFE

TRIANGLE:
BALANCED AND DEEP
RELATIONSHIPS

SQUARE:
MULTIPLYING
MISSIONAL DISCIPLES

PENTAGON:
PERSONAL CALLING

UP
WORSHIP

HEXAGON:
PRAYER

HEPTAGON:
COMMUNAL
SPIRITUAL HEALTH

OUT
PERSON OF PEACE/
EVANGELISM

IN
FELLOWSHIP

POP TRIANGLE:
RELATIONAL MISSION

- Is there a LifeShape that would meet the Context need?

- Is there something specific they need to learn about the Bible that would meet the Context need?

- Is there something in my spiritual DNA that would meet the Context need?

- Is it something else?

I'm discerning that the next Content tool is:

_____

_____

_____

_____

_____

_____

_____

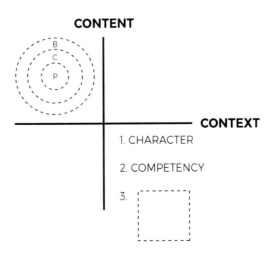

INTERVAL 7
PERSONAL CALLING

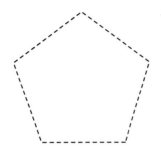

Helpful plans for personal calling:

- Have the participants identify what phases they have experienced in the past and what they've learned.

- Identify someone whose base ministry is the same as yours. How can they learn from that person?

- Have participant identify ways in which churches have sought to plug them into a system rather than see what God might be releasing them into.

- Identify areas that they avoid and refuse to learn in their weaknesses, which are opportunities for growth.

WEEK 1
CONTENT TOOL

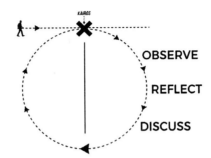

BEFORE HUDDLE

Have participants read the chapter on the Pentagon in *Building a Discipling Culture*. Make sure they are ready to share what most grabbed their attention and served as their Kairos.

NOTES:

- The majority of this Huddle will be discussion-oriented. At this point, you don't want to get to the "What is God saying to me?" part of the discussion. That will come next week. You can take them around the first half of the Learning Circle, helping them to Observe, Reflect, and Discuss.

- The emphasis from this tool must be on IDENTITY. It's about who God has shaped you to be, not what others want you to be or even who you think you should be.

- There are many psychological approaches to identifying and understanding our identity (i.e. Myers Briggs, Strengths Finder, etc). The Pentagon is a biblical approach to the same.

- We are called to be like Jesus, a balanced expression of each grace. We cannot excuse ourselves from growing in the graces we are less comfortable with.

- God uses relationships and circumstances to challenge us to grow in the areas where we are less comfortable

ASSIGNMENT FOR NEXT HUDDLE

Have them take the free 5-fold test online at fivefoldsurvey.com and bring their results to the next Huddle.

WEEK 2
PERSONAL

BRIEF HUDDLE OUTLINE:

1. Teach the Pentagon in four minutes or less. Remember that in the following Huddle, one of them will be teaching it, so give them something they can imitate.

2. Have them take out the results from the fivefoldsurvey.com online test. Remember, these results DO NOT tell them which of the Fivefold ministries they are. It gives a snapshot of *what they are currently expressing*. It will probably provide insight into what their Base ministry could be, as well as what Phase they might be operating out of.

3. Connecting the Kairos they had from the previous Huddle, walk the participants around the Learning Circle, paying close attention to the Reflect and Discuss portion. You will probably need to help them see how you see them, what you notice about them, and what you see God doing in them. Give them lots of encouragement!

4. As always, make sure they are able to clearly identify what they believe God is saying and what they need to do about it.

NOTES:

- Your highest score does not necessarily reflect your true base ministry. It is however likely one of your top two scores.

- As a leader, be able to describe each of the five ministries through the lens of your own experience.

- A helpful metaphor that allows people to identify which is their base ministry:

- When building a house, the Apostle will have vision for where to build and what kind of house to build. Apostles build where others haven't.

- Prophets will have a sense from the Lord about the significance of what the house is for and what God may be doing through the process of creating a new house. Prophets will also be sensitive to any emerging threats to the project.

- Evangelists fall in love with the vision of the house and desire to connect (sell) others to the vision. They just can't imagine that others wouldn't love the opportunity to buy this new house!

- Pastors are most interested in making sure those who will live in the house are cared for well. After all, the house is only as valuable as the people living inside it.

- Teachers will have the blueprints out on the tables ensuring the house is made to specifications and that every last detail is accounted for. After all, caring for the new residents means caring for the their new residence.

Coaching Tip:

Often people will try to be what they believe culture wants them to be, who they think they *should* be, rather than who God *created* them to be.

WEEK 3
LEADERSHIP

BRIEF HUDDLE OUTLINE:

1. Take two minutes and have each person report out if he or she followed through on his or her plan.

2. Have one of the participants teach the Pentagon in four minutes or less.

3. Using the Pentagon, identify the base ministries for each of the people they are leading either in the group they are leading or in their family. Does your team represent both sides of the Pioneer/ Developer spectrum? Are people serving out of their Base or are they suffering from the "plug-and-play" mentality?

4. Mine out the Kairos and walk them around the Learning Circle so that each of them knows what God is saying and what they are going to do about it.

NOTES:

*   There is no golden rule that you need all five ministries perfectly represented on a team for the team to be wonderfully effective. This exercise simply challenges the leaders to be more aware of who God has placed around them and how often we tend to resist those who are least like us.

- It is wise to surround ourselves with others who are not like us. We desperately need the other voices to help balance our perspective. (At best, we only represent 3/5 of God's perspective on any given issue!)

WEEK 4
CHARACTER / SKILLS QUESTIONS

BRIEF HUDDLE OUTLINE:

1. Take two minutes and have each person report out on whether he or she followed through on his or her plan.

2. Have everyone turn to the Character/Skills questions. Pair them up. Then, give each of them 3-5 minutes of time to develop an exercise using the questions that they will lead their partner through. This will help them develop an exercise on their own in a safe environment and also teach them to lead someone through the Learning Circle with these questions.

3. Have each pair walk each other through their exercise and the Learning Circle.

4. Have each person share what their exercise was and why he or she picked it. What you want to notice is their level of discernment.

5. Give affirmation and critique based on your observations and reflections of their leading each other, their level of discernment, etc.

Coaching Tip:

Question: How many people in your Huddle have started a Huddle of their own yet? How close to ready are the people who haven't? Now is the time to help them start leaving he nest.

IMPORTANT FOR NEXT HUDDLE

The next Huddle will be going out on mission together with a twist: As much as possible, have each participant bring ONE PERSON in whom they are looking to invest (or already are investing) for this mission experience. Use any easier missional OUT, but still with a degree of challenge. Make sure you have the details ironed out for what that means for the upcoming Huddle

WEEK 5
MISSION

THINGS TO CONSIDER:

- This can't be an optional week for anyone. You want everyone in the group to be growing in this competency.

- Hypothetically, your participants will bring along one person in whom they are looking to invest (or already are investing) to share this experience with them.

- Page 179 of this guide has a list of suggestions and ideas for what it can look like to do mission together as a Huddle.

- After doing mission, make sure the Huddle has time to process what God is saying.

HELPFUL COACHING TIP

The sixth, seventh, and eighth LifeShapes are simply the "how-to's" of the Triangle. We've found this little insight to be very helpful in people remembering the purpose of each of these tools.

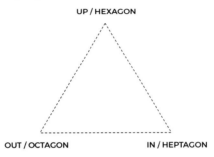

- The Hexagon, which is about prayer, helps us understand how to do UP.

- The Heptagon, which is about spiritual communal health, helps us understand how to do IN.

- The Octagon, which is about relational mission, helps us understand how to do OUT.

- In addition, our latest feedback shows us that it can be harder for some Huddles to grasp the Heptagon and the Octagon. Feel the freedom to find other ways to dive deeper into how to do IN and OUT with your Huddle.

- The third edition of *Building a Discipling Culture* shows how to talk about the Person of Peace using the Triangle, instead of through the Octagon. Consider this approach with your Huddle, and pick the option that fits your needs best.

INTERVAL 8
PRAYER

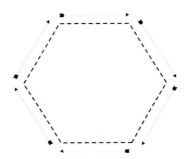

Helpful plans for prayer:

- Read Richard Foster's book on Prayer.

- See the exercises we've listed for each week.

- Take a prayer retreat, a day by yourself, splitting the day into the six portions of the Lord's Prayer.

- Take each of the six phrases and find three scriptures for each that have been significant in your understanding of that phrase.

WEEK 1
CONTENT TOOL

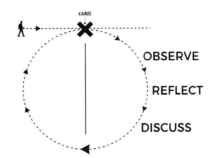

BEFORE HUDDLE

Have participants read the chapter on the Hexagon in *Building a Discipling Culture*. Make sure they are ready to share what most grabbed their attention and served as their Kairos.

NOTES:

- The majority of this Huddle will be discussion- oriented. At this point, you don't want to get to the "What is God saying to me?" part of the discussion. That will come next week. Instead, take them around the first half of the Learning Circle, helping them to Observer, Reflect, and Discuss.

- Many have recited this prayer since childhood and know it only as a form of liturgy. But this prayer was given to the disciples (and to us) to **keep the main thing the main thing**. Our daily prayer and lifestyle is to be about God's Kingdom, his will, being established on earth (Genesis 1:27-28). His promise is to give us, his chosen representatives, access to everything we need each day to accomplish what he asks of us, even in the face of the enemy's assault.

- This prayer is our motto, our creed, our mantra, our vision, our values, our invitation, and our challenge

ASSIGNMENT FOR NEXT HUDDLE

Have them begin each day using the lens of the Lord's Prayer to filter their day. Imagine the Hexagon is a filter and pour a concern or question through it, allowing your issue to pass through each phrase. How did your perspective on the issue change as it passed through the filter? Have them ready to share a Kairos based on this prayer exercise.

WEEK 2
PERSONAL

BRIEF HUDDLE OUTLINE:

1. Teach the Hexagon in four minutes or less. Remember that in the following Huddle, one of them will be teaching it, so give them something they can imitate.

2. Tell the group that some of them will be helping to lead the Huddle tonight. Two people at a time are going to share their Kairos from doing the prayer exercise, and you are going to pick someone else to walk each of them through the Learning Circle, straight through what God is saying to them and what they are going to do about it.

3. Have two people share their Kairos from the prayer exercise, and then choose one person to lead the Huddle by walking them around the Learning Circle.

4. Use that rhythm again until everyone has shared his or her Kairos.

5. Take time to give affirmation and critique for those who led people through the Learning Circle. Cast vision again for beginning Huddles for those who haven't yet.

NOTES:

- The more we practice this prayer as a filter for issues in our life, the more we will find our general perspective changing to reflect the powerful truths of the prayer.

- Prayer is the practice of having our perspective changed to God's.

- Prayer is learning to represent our Father who is also the King. We must know how the King rules if we are to represent him with clarity and confidence.

- You can be good at prayer or bad at prayer in the same way that you can be good or bad at communicating with your spouse, friends, or kids.

Coaching Tip:
As people are helping to lead the Huddle, note your observations. What are they doing well? Where is there room for improvement? Having notes to go back to is really helpful.

WEEK 3
LEADERSHIP

BRIEF HUDDLE OUTLINE:

1. Take two minutes and have each person report out if he or she followed through on his or her plan.

2. Have one of the participants teach the Hexagon in four minutes or less.

3. Using the Hexagon, have each participant assess the group they are leading on a scale of 1-10 for each of the 6 areas of the Lord's Prayer (Father, King, Provision, Forgiveness, Protection, Deliverance). For each area, ask this question, "On a scale of 1-10, how does my group experience/express God as Father?" Then do the same for each of the other areas. What was their high? Celebrate it. What was their low?

4. Have two people share their Kairos moments from the exercise, and choose one other person to lead the Huddle by walking them around the Learning Circle.

5. Use that rhythm again until everyone has shared his or her Kairos.

6. Take time to give affirmation and critique for those who led people through the Learning Circle.

NOTES:

- Remember the Lord's Prayer reflects the UP, IN, OUT dimensions. Father/King (UP), Provision/Forgiveness (IN), Protection/ Deliverance (OUT).

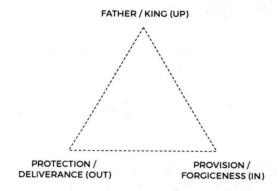

WEEK 4
CHARACTER / SKILLS
QUESTIONS

BRIEF HUDDLE OUTLINE:

1. Take two minutes and have each person report out on whether he or she followed through on his or her plan.

2. Intro: One important component of building Character is faithfulness and recognizing that, while we hope to see the results our hearts long for, real Kingdom results are always left in our Father's hands.

3. Exercise: What is one area that you need to continue to seek breakthrough in through prayer that you're tempted not to continue pressing into? Have each person share.

4. Continued exercise: Sometimes, as in the story of the paralytic who is lowered through the roof to be put in front of Jesus, we need people to leverage their faith for us (like the paralytic). At other times, we leverage our collective faith for someone else (like the paralytic's friends).

5. Spend time praying as a group for each person's place where they are seeking breakthrough, going from one person to the next.

IMPORTANT FOR NEXT HUDDLE

The next Huddle will be going out on mission together, so make sure your group has all the details they need. On this endeavor, you as the leader will be coming up with your own idea for what the group will go out and do.

Coaching Tip:

This exercise is really helpful as you seek the collective breakthrough together as a group. It's definitely one worth returning to from time to time.

WEEK 5
MISSION

THINGS TO CONSIDER:

- This can't be an optional week for anyone. You want everyone in the group to be growing in this competency.

- **Come up with a missional endeavor of your own.** Thinking through where your Huddle is based on this interval on Prayer, what is an appropriate missional exercise for your Huddle to go out and do together?

- After doing mission, make sure the Huddle has time to process what God is saying.

Coaching Tip:
This week you will be coming up with a missional endeavor on your own. Be creative!

DISCERNMENT EXERCISE

WHERE SHOULD THE HUDDLE GO NEXT?

CONTEXT: Evaluate the people in your group and the group as a whole

- Where are they on the Square right now?

  _____

  _____

  _____

- What Character weaknesses are there right now? Strengths?

  _____

  _____

  _____

- What Competency weaknesses are there right now? Strengths?

  _____

  _____

  _____

- Discern: Based on these questions and my reflections, I think God is saying my group needs to learn

  _____

  _____

  _____

CONTENT: What Content fits what my group needs to learn next?

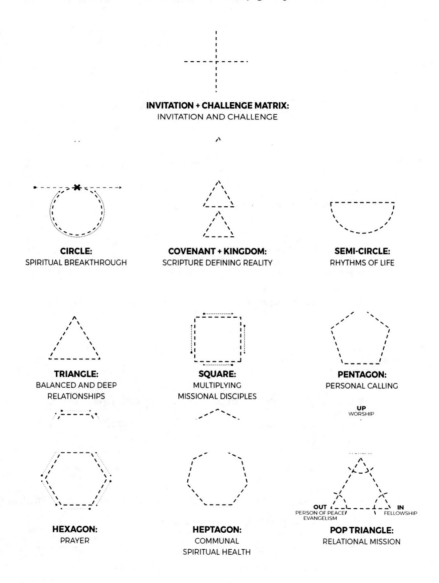

INVITATION + CHALLENGE MATRIX:
INVITATION AND CHALLENGE

CIRCLE:
SPIRITUAL BREAKTHROUGH

COVENANT + KINGDOM:
SCRIPTURE DEFINING REALITY

SEMI-CIRCLE:
RHYTHMS OF LIFE

TRIANGLE:
BALANCED AND DEEP
RELATIONSHIPS

SQUARE:
MULTIPLYING
MISSIONAL DISCIPLES

PENTAGON:
PERSONAL CALLING

HEXAGON:
PRAYER

HEPTAGON:
COMMUNAL
SPIRITUAL HEALTH

UP
WORSHIP

OUT
PERSON OF PEACE/
EVANGELISM

IN
FELLOWSHIP

POP TRIANGLE:
RELATIONAL MISSION

- Is there a LifeShape that would meet the Context need?

- Is there something specific they need to learn about the Bible that would meet the Context need?

- Is there something in my spiritual DNA that would meet the Context need?

- Is it something else?

I'm discerning that the next Content tool is:

_____

_____

_____

_____

_____

_____

_____

_____

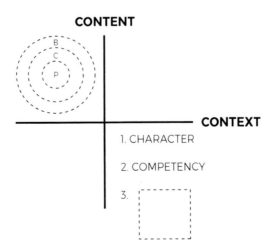

INTERVAL 9
COMMUNAL SPIRITUAL HEALTH

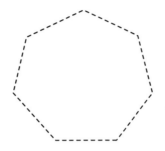

Helpful plans for communal spiritual health:

- Read through the book of Acts and identify where you see these seven elements expressed.

  Note that our experience over the past 10 years shows us that some Huddles have more trouble grasping this shape than the others. Discern where your Huddle is and what they need with this shape. Should it take more time? Should it wait until year two? Be flexible and use this shape in the most helpful way for your group.

WEEK 1
CONTENT TOOL

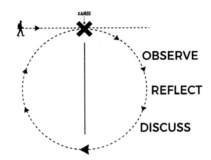

OBSERVE

REFLECT

DISCUSS

BEFORE HUDDLE

Have participants read the appendix on the Heptagon in *Building a Discipling Culture*. Make sure they are ready to share what most grabbed their attention and served as their Kairos.

Coaching Tip:

From this point of your Huddle, feel free to have participants lead the whole Huddle or pieces of one, always engaging in affirmation and critique. Also, allow the group into your process for discerning where the group is going and let them into that decision-making process.

NOTES:

- The majority of this Huddle will be discussion-oriented. At this point, you don't want to get to the "What is God saying to me?" part of the discussion. That will come next week. Instead, you can take them around the first half of the Learning Circle, helping them to Observer, Reflect, and Discuss.

Coaching Tip:

What this tool can give us is a lens for understanding the role of the Holy Spirit in the life of our group.

WEEK 2
PERSONAL

BRIEF HUDDLE OUTLINE:

1. Teach the Heptagon in four minutes or less. Remember that in the following Huddle, one of them will be teaching it, so give them something they can imitate.

2. Have each participant measure themselves for each of the seven areas on a scale of 1–10.

3. Give them a minute of silence to think through their Kairos from last Huddle as well as their reflections on their measurements. What's the big Kairos?

4. Walk the participants around the Learning Circle so that by the close of the Huddle each participant is able to clearly articulate what God is saying and what he or she is going to do about it.

NOTES:

- Which tools would you encourage for growth in each category (e.g. Nutrition: Do you have a regular rhythm (Semi-Circle) of bible study?)

- Can you explain how the different categories relate to each other? Connect MRS GREN to the Semi-Circle. Nutrition and Respiration help us REST/ABIDE, which increase sensitivity and movement. The bi-product of movement in response to the Spirit is growth and reproduction — PRODUCTION/ FRUITFULNESS. Excretion forces the return to the posture of REST/ABIDING from which everything else flows.

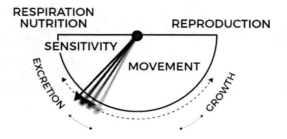

WEEK 3
LEADERSHIP

BRIEF HUDDLE OUTLINE:

1. Take two minutes and have each person report out on whether he or she followed through on his or her plan.

2. Teach the Heptagon on top of the Semi-Circle in four minutes or less. Use the image from the leader guide on the previous page for a starting point.

3. Using the Heptagon, have each participant assess the group they are leading on a scale of 1-10 for each of the seven areas. What was their high? Celebrate it. What was their low? What's the Kairos?

4. Have two people share their Kairos from the exercise, and then choose one person to lead the Huddle by walking them around the Learning Circle. Interject when necessary.

5. Use that rhythm again until everyone has shared his or her Kairos.

6. Take time to give affirmation and critique for those who led people through the Learning Circle.

NOTES:

• It's always helpful to remember leaders define culture. This usually keeps us from putting all the responsibility for poor results on our people. This is often the most painful reflection in parenting: "My kids are much of what I invested in them."

Coaching Tip:

Remember that all of the LifeShapes serve as excellent analytical tools that can give us helpful windows into what is happening around us. Looking through the lens of the Kingdom helps us calibrate our life to the life of the Kingdom. Like any lens, when you put on a pair of glasses, what wasn't clear before suddenly becomes clear.

WEEK 4
CHARACTER / SKILLS QUESTIONS

BRIEF HUDDLE OUTLINE:

1. Take two minutes and have each person report out on whether he or she followed through on his or her plan.

2. Have the participants turn to the Character/Skills questions.

3. Give them two minutes to read through all of the Skills questions and then ask, "What is God challenging you to do that you may not want to?"

4. Allow them each to answer, helping them identify the Kairos. Then walk them around the Learning Circle, making sure each person articulates what God is saying and what they are going to do about it.

Coaching Tip:
We have found the phrase "missional eyes" helpful in allowing people to understand how they can see the world through the lens of the Kingdom.

IMPORTANT FOR NEXT HUDDLE

Between now and the next Huddle, have each person think through either a physical place (a neighborhood, coffee shop, etc.) or a network (college students, artists, etc.) that God might be calling them to reach out to in mission. Before the next Huddle, have them spend 1-2 hours in the place of that physical place or where people from those networks would hang out. Have them write down their observations of being there and what the Holy Spirit was showing them as they look at this place with missional eyes.

WEEK 5
MISSION

This time, the Huddle will be gathering in your normal gathering spot because you will be processing the Kairos moments you've had in already engaging in a mission listening exercise in the previous week.

BRIEF HUDDLE OUTLINE:

1. Take two minutes and have each person report out if he or she followed through on his or her plan from the Skills Kairos in the previous week.

2. Give each person 2-3 minutes to share about his or her missional excursion to either the network or neighborhood where they spent some time "listening" the previous week. Have each person identify his or her big Kairos.

3. Is there a collective Kairos the group is having that can be walked around the Learning Circle? Are there a couple of themes emerging? Whatever it is, walk the group around the Learning Circle.

NOTES:

*   At this point, people should be thinking not just about who they are discipling, but also about how they can lead the people they are discipling into mission together. That's the purpose of this exercise.

INTERVAL 10
RELATIONAL MISSION

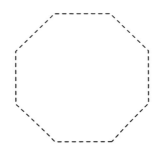

Helpful plans for relational mission:

- Have each participant write down one Person of Peace (or a couple) into whom they want to invest their time, energy and prayers.

- Identify places in your life where each of the eight elements are already happening (and not happening).

- Go through the book of Acts. Where do the eight elements play out?

- Note that our experience over the past 10 years shows us that some Huddles have more trouble grasping this shape than the others. Discern where your Huddle is and what they need with this shape. Should it take more time? Should it wait until year two? Be flexible and use this shape in the most helpful way for your group.

- In addition, you may consider using the triangle from the

"Relational Mission" chapter of Building a Discipling Culture instead of the Octagon as you consider the Person of Peace.

WEEK 1
CONTENT TOOL

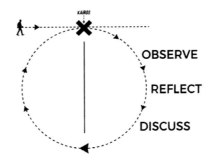

BEFORE HUDDLE

Have participants read the chapter on the Octagon in *Building a Discipling Culture*. Make sure they are ready to share what most grabbed their attention and served as their Kairos.

NOTES:

- A Person of Peace (POP) is someone who likes you, likes your vision/mission, and wants to serve your vision/ mission.

- Encourage participants to identify people in their lives who fit this description.

- We can apply the POP strategy both in reaching out to non-Christians as well as in discerning those Christians who make good team

WEEK 2
PERSONAL

BRIEF HUDDLE OUTLINE:

1. Teach the Octagon (or the Person of Peace in relation to the Triangle) in five minutes or less. Remember that in the following Huddle, one of them will be teaching it, so give them something they can imitate.

2. Have each participant share one story that exemplifies the Person of Peace already at work in their life.

3. Give them a minute of silence to think through their Kairos from last Huddle as well as from this week. What's the big Kairos?

4. Walk the participants around the Learning Circle so that by the close of the Huddle, each participant is able to clearly articulate what God is saying and what he or she is going to do about it.

NOTES:

- It's helpful to stress that much of these happen in the course of our lives. Too often we get so wrapped in what we're doing in life we forget there is a world going on all around us. We need to open our eyes when we're sitting in the coffee shop, at the grocery store, at the bank, on the plane, at a dinner, in the park, etc.

WEEK 3
LEADERSHIP

BRIEF HUDDLE OUTLINE:

1. Take two minutes and have each person report out on whether he or she followed through on his or her plan.

2. Have a participant teach the Octagon in five minutes or less.

3. If you're using the Octagon, have each participant assess the group they are leading on a scale of 1-10 for each of the eight areas. What was their high? Celebrate it. What was their low? What's the Kairos?

4. Rather than going completely around the Learning Circle, go for more in-depth discussion, using this as a key moment for you to do some impromptu teaching and answer questions, to wrestle with these concepts for the things they are leading, etc.

5. You can tell them that for this Huddle, they aren't going to be expected to articulate, "What is God saying and what am I going to do about it?" It's more about the discussion and in-depth teaching and insights you provide as the leader.

NOTES:

*   Notice how what we see in the book of Acts is the Early Church using the exact same strategy that Jesus gives the 12 and then the

72 in Luke 9 and 10. This is Jesus being as directive you'll find on strategy and practice.

- Knowing your group, what do you think might be key teaching inputs you can give during the discussion time? You might want to prepare and think through these things in advance.

WEEK 4
CHARACTER / SKILLS
QUESTIONS

IMPORTANT HUDDLE NOTE:

There will be some brief role-playing tonight that will allow people to experiment sharing the Gospel in a safe place. This will be a very training-specific Huddle.

BRIEF HUDDLE OUTLINE:

1. Tell everyone up front that tonight you are going to engage in a training exercise that will allow us to experiment and try sharing the Gospel in different ways and that this Huddle is all about training in a safe place. This Huddle is going to be about the skill of sharing your faith.

2. Content note: People tend to gravitate more toward the Covenantal side of the Gospel (relationship) or the Kingdom side of it (being part of a bigger story), meaning people come to faith in different ways. Discipleship is the process that connects us to the second theme that may not, at the outset, call out to us as much.

3. Give them two minutes of silence to think through the missional place to which God might be calling them to lead a team of disciples. Is this mission group going to connect more to Covenant or Kingdom? Then engage in discussion, allowing each person to share his or her thoughts. Give feedback and challenge as needed. Make sure you share yours as well.

4. What would Good News look like for this context through the lens of Covenant or the lens of Kingdom? Give them three minutes to write down a 3-4 sentence proclamation of Good News for this mission context through the lens of Covenant or Kingdom that is best suited for their context. Make sure you share yours as well, but connect your personal story into as well so it isn't just theory. How is resurrection playing into your life?

5. Have each person share what he or she has written, and then give feedback.

6. Get them get in pairs and have them role-play as if they were sharing the Good News with someone in that missional context. Have the person playing opposite them push back a little, ask questions, engage, etc.

7. With a partner, model for the whole group what one of these conversations could look like.

8. Have someone volunteer to role-play in front of the whole group, and then give affirmation and critique.

9. Give them their assignment for the next Huddle.

SAMPLE LANGUAGE:

- **Covenant:** God is your Father and he loves you. He's so close to you that you can almost reach out and touch him. He believes in you. He wants good things for you. And through the death and resurrection of Jesus, you can know him. Do you want to know him like I know him?

- **Kingdom:** God is putting the whole world back together. All of it. He's restoring it to how he originally created it to be, from the brokenness in me all the way to broken and unjust systems that exist. And he wants us to get in on it. Through the death and resurrection of Jesus, God wants to use us in his story of rescuing the whole world. Do you want to join in on the movement we're part of?

NOTES:

- Remember, we aren't talking about going out and sharing this Gospel proclamation with everyone. We are looking for God to reveal Persons of Peace to us who are ready to hear it. What this exercise allows us to do is "be ready to give a reason for the hope that we have, both in season and out of season. But do so with gentleness and respect." (1 Peter 3:15) This is about being ready when the situation arises.

- It will feel rough for people as they are struggling to articulate something deep inside of them. Expect it to take more than one night for them to feel comfortable. It may actually take a good deal of time.

ASSIGNMENT FOR NEXT HUDDLE

Between now and the next Huddle, everyone should have a conversation with one Person of Peace, sharing what he or she tried in Huddle. They can do it using this lens when they talk to the Person of Peace:

"I'm trying to better explain my faith to people because I think a lot of people actually widely misunderstand what Jesus was up to. Would you mind if I tried explaining it to you for two minutes and then you give me some feedback on what made sense, what didn't, and any questions you'd ask?"

What this does is create a situation to put the Person of Peace at ease as well as freedom for the Huddle participant to try something new and not worry about the results or consequences. The purpose isn't to lead them to faith right then and there; the purpose is to have a go at sharing their faith! either a physical place (a neighborhood, coffee shop, etc.) or a network (college students, artists, etc.) that God might be calling them to reach

WEEK 5
MISSION

DIFFERENT MISSION WEEK

This time, the Huddle will be gathering in your normal gathering spot as you will be processing the Kairos moments you've had engaging your Persons of Peace in sharing your faith.

BRIEF HUDDLE OUTLINE:

1. Have each person share how their experience sharing their faith with a Person of Peace went.

2. Have each person share what he or she learned, what excited him or her, what made him or her anxious, and where he or she believes there is room for improvement.

PART 3

AFTER YEAR 1
+ APPENDIX

WHAT DO WE DO IN HUDDLE AFTER THE YEAR 1 FRAMEWORK IS COMPLETE?

Remember that Huddle is the context in which you continue to invest into missional leaders, providing support and encouragement as well as challenge and accountability. You will continue to process with them what God is saying to them and what they are going to do about it and to invest in them in ways that are appropriate to where they are on their leadership journey.

In other words, just because the Year 1 framework is complete, it doesn't mean that God has stopped talking to them or conforming them to the likeness of Christ! You will continue to seek the Character and Competency of Jesus formed in them.

What we hope the Year 1 framework has taught you how to discern what Content is needed for the Context of their current leadership journey. That was the purpose of the Discernment exercises throughout the framework.

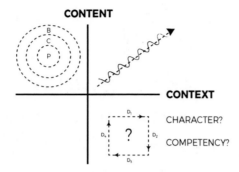

- What are the leaders I'm investing in facing right now? What is the context of their lives and their leadership journey?

- What content needs to be inputted based on this?

Obviously, the framework we gave for the Year 1 framework can be continually used as you discern the content that is needed for the context of their leadership journey:

THE FRAMEWORK

WEEK 1:	WEEK 2:	WEEK 3:	WEEK 4:	WEEK 5:
CONTENT TOOL	PERSONAL	LEADERSHIP	CHARACTER/ SKILL QUESTIONS	MISSION

Here are a few examples of Content tools you might discern would be helpful:

- Kairos from their current leadership context
- Nicene or Apostles Creed
- Missional practices
- Fasting
- Study on the book of James

The possibilities are endless.

However, you might also find this framework is not flexible enough from Huddle to Huddle, and so you may desire a season of far more flexibility. Again, this framework is a helpful guide, but it isn't law. We want each Huddle leader to be able to wisely discern the following:

- What is God trying to accomplish in this group in this season?

- What does God need us to do in this specific Huddle today to faithfully live into that season?

Sometimes that will look like adhering to the framework we have provided; sometimes that will look like stepping completely outside of it.

Our experience is that by staying within the framework of Year 1 and doing the discernment exercises teaches Huddle leaders this skill set. **However, we do feel it is important to regularly return to the Character and Skills questions as they continually orient us around the three dimensions of Jesus' life. We constantly need recalibration, and these questions help us attend to that.**

Above all, remember that the people in your Huddle should all be leading something, and that will provide the context for what you are investing. Trust us, if they are all hitting the brick wall of D2 in leading a Missional Community, that's what you're going to be teaching them. The experience of mistakes and not knowing what to do next shapes them to be people who want to learn about very specific things. And it's in that crucible of frustration that Jesus is also shaping their character.

HOW OFTEN DO WE MEET AFTER THE FIRST YEAR?

The general rule is that the more you meet, the more ability you have to shape the lives of the people you are investing in. However, you get to a point where leading away from meeting in the group every week is actually a more shaping experience. Think through it this way: The more you trust the people in what they are leading, the less "official" Huddle time they need.

Many Huddles go to every other week in their second year. But on the other hand, never go less than once a month meeting together.

APPENDIX

HUDDLE ON MISSION TOGETHER

Here are a few examples of how you can use Huddle as a missional training ground for the people you are discipling. It is assumed that with each missional excursion, you will create space to learn from the experience as we discern what God is saying to us and what we should do about it:

- Have everyone come to Huddle at the normal place, but have each person bring $5. (They don't know why.) Each person is then assigned to go spend that money at a restaurant/coffee shop somewhere, buy a drink, ask the Holy Spirit to reveal to them a person of peace and have ONE substantive conversation in the one hour they are there. It doesn't have to be Jesus-related, but it should be something deep.

- Go out for dinner one night with your Huddle and have everyone bring his or her Persons of Peace.

- Have everyone in the Huddle bring their families (if applicable) and invite Persons of Peace with their families to the park for a cookout and family games.

- Have every person in the Huddle share your communities' language for the gospel with one Person of Peace to whom they are close. Have them explain to the POP that they are simply practicing and are neither asking for or expecting a response. Have the POP give feedback. Did it make sense? What questions would they have? Did they feel pressured? Make sure to process in Huddle.

- Have the Huddle regularly serve with the poor and regularly process in Huddle.

- Move into bolder expressions of mission with your Huddle. Set up a "Free Prayer Table" on the sidewalk of a crowded street or shopping center and offer prayer to people as they pass.

- Have everyone in the Huddle commit to praying for one specific Person of Peace every time they are in Huddle and have them commit to pray frequently in their own prayer times until they see breakthrough. Process the Kairos of frustration and breakthrough in Huddle.

- Have everyone in the Huddle meet during lunch on a workday and go to a place where people are and engage in random acts of kindness.

- Have the Huddle meeting in a public place like a restaurant or coffee shop and use the time to pray for people in the place, asking for the Holy Spirit to show someone who is a Person of Peace and engage appropriately.

- Use one of your Huddles as a time to practice sharing the gospel in a relational way. Allow time for feedback, encouragement, coaching, and critique.

- Use your Huddle time to explore the differences between Persons of Peace who are passing relationships (meet them randomly) and permanent relationships (they are a regular part of your life). How is mission done with these different types of POPs?

- Have everyone in your Huddle knock on five doors of people living around them bringing cookies and engage in conversation. Follow up with a dinner invitation if the relationship seems ready.

- Have everyone in the Huddle ask God: 1) what missional context they should be trying to reach into, and 2) what should the gospel touch point for that missional context be. Share in Huddle and then have their plans respond appropriately.

CHARACTER QUESTIONS

UP

Do I make enough space for prayer?

Do I pursue intimacy with Jesus?

What is on my heart for intercession?

Am I living in the power of the Spirit?

Am I seeing personal revival?

Do I still feel pleasure?

Am I living in a state of peace? Am I afraid or nervous?

Am I obedient to God's prompting?

IN

Do I love the flock?

Is time a blessing or a curse?

Am I resting enough?

How are my relationships with my friends?

Am I experiencing intimacy in relationships?

Do I keep my promises?

How easy is it for me to trust people?

Am I discipling others? Is my family happy?

Am I sleeping/eating well?

Am I making myself vulnerable to others?

OUT

Do I have a heart for the lost?

How often do I share my faith?

Do I leave time for relationships with non-Christians?

Am I running the race with perseverance?

Do I have a vision?

Am I looking after the least of these? (the poor, vulnerable, forgotten)

Am I dying to success?

Am I proud or ashamed of the Gospel?

Am I a servant?

Do I find it easy to recognize people of peace? Can I take risks?

SKILLS QUESTIONS

UP

Is the worship in my group dynamic and full of intimacy?

Do I find it easy to receive guidance for the next step in the life of my group?

How easy is it to talk to a whole group "from the front"?

Can I teach effectively from God's word?

Does my group share the vision God has given me?

Do I feel relaxed about leading times of Holy Spirit ministry?

IN

Do members of my group feel cared for? Am I effective at resolving conflict?

Do I take on the discipline of confrontation?

Have I defined my own boundaries well?

Am I flexible?

How are my weaknesses as a leader compensated for by others?

How do I cope with over-dependent people?

How do I cope with controlling group members?

Are there difficulties in my relationships with co-leaders/assistant leaders?

OUT

Is my group growing?

Am I too controlling as a leader?

How welcoming is my group to new people?

Can all group members identify at least one Person of Peace?

Am I using leaders in my group effectively?

Do I find it easy to multiply groups?

Are those I am discipling turning into effective leaders?

Is my group effective in regularly doing OUT activity?

Does my group have a single people group in mind?

COVENANT
AND KINGDOM

The following is a excerpt from Mike Breen's book, *Covenant and Kingdom: The DNA of the Bible*. This will briefly outline the main concepts explored in understanding these two themes of scripture. For a much greater look into these ideas, feel free to pick up the book, available in paperback or ebook.

As Jesus reveals his relationship with his heavenly Father, Jesus invites us into a new depth of understanding of the Covenant. He offers to us the relationship that he enjoys with the Father.

FATHER

John's gospel—the gospel of the Covenant—defines the relationship that exists between God the Father and the Son. The Son is revealed as Jesus throughout the gospel.

Jesus says that he does only what he sees the Father doing (John 5:19). In shared identity, common purpose is forged. As his disciples mature in their relationship with him, Jesus reveals that they will share in a common relationship with the one that he calls Father and that together they will fashion the cords that will hold the Covenant together:

> "If anyone loves me, he will obey my teaching. My Father will love him, and we will come to him and make our home with him." (John 14:23)

Jesus came as one who was and is in radical, deep and intimate Covenant with the God of heaven. Today, he draws people to himself and builds a community of people who follow him, who want to become more like him and enter more into the realities of the Covenant that Jesus shares with his Father.

IDENTITY

Identity flows from the one who gives us life. We are children of God, born again into a new family, given a new name and a new identity by which we can gain access to all of the resources of our Covenant partner. The New Testament teaches that when we are baptized we embrace our new identity. Jesus connects us to God and defines who we are. We bear his Name, and everything he has is ours. Our identity is so caught up with God's that the New Testament is able to say that we are heirs of heaven and co-heirs with Christ. God's commitment to us is written indelibly in the blood of Jesus. As we share in the Covenant meal that Jesus gave, the bread and wine help us to remember who he is and who we are.

OBEDIENCE

The New Covenant means that God's code of behavior for his people— "the Law"—is now written in our hearts. This happens when the Holy Spirit fills us and gives us new life when we are born again as God's children. Now we are free to obey God because this is truly a reflection of who we are. We choose to obey because this is the most consistent way of expressing our identity. What we do tells the world who we are:

> "If you love me, you will obey what I command." (John 14:15)

Obedience is always an act of love. Because of our shared Covenant identity with Jesus, we do the things he did:

> "I tell you the truth, anyone who has faith in me will do what I have been doing. He will do even greater things than these, because I am going to the Father." (John 14:12)

Exercising this life of Covenant oneness means living a life of security and confidence:

> "And I will do whatever you ask in my name, so that the Son may bring glory to the Father. You may ask me for anything in my name, and I will do it." (John 14:13-14)

It may be helpful to sum this up visually in the same way that we did in the Old Testament Summary:

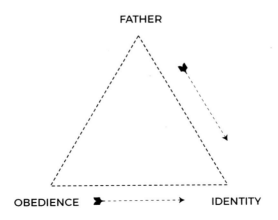

FATHER

OBEDIENCE   IDENTITY

The Covenant begins with the Father, who gives us our identity. Now we are able to obey because as children of God we are empowered to do so. At times, we may find ourselves seeking to approach God through obedience rather than in simple recognition of our identity. When we do this, we fall into the trap of the Pharisees whom Jesus encountered. As we are God's children, he is already pleased with us, and this knowledge liberates us from the legalistic observance that so often leads to frustration and guilt.

SUMMARY OF KINGDOM IN THE NEW TESTAMENT

It is not with a show of majestic judgment that Jesus revealed the Kingship of God. Rather, it was with servant-hearted tenderness toward us, his wayward subjects. His sacrificial love brought the ultimate victory of the Kingdom over our enemies of sin, death and hell.

Until the birth of Jesus, the prophets foresaw only the coming of the King. But now the King has come among us. The King of heaven has taken on flesh and has chosen to walk among his wayward subjects, to reveal the future he has prepared for us, a future that we can taste now if only we will surrender to his Kingship.

In almost every expression of earthly kingdom, the monarch benefits most from its existence. With the Kingdom of heaven, however, the Kingdom is for the subjects. The King is a servant King who wants his people to be the greatest recipients of its benefits. In response to receiving all the blessings, the people of the King offer him their love and loyalty, glory and honor.

Again the Kingdom (or Kingship) of God is expressed in three key words: King, authority and power.